D1553085

"Stop That Dog Now!"

An Owner's Guide to a Problem Free Dog

by Sue Clauss

First published by Dog Ear Publishing
4010 W. 86th Street, Ste H
Indianapolis, IN 46268
www.dogearpublishing.net

ISBN: 1-59858-246-1
Library of Congress Control Number: 2006937646

This book is printed on acid-free paper.

Printed in the United States of America

Acknowledgments

I would like to sincerely thank the following for their contributions to my career and thus this book:

Terry Wright
Janet Long
William Koehler
Job Michael Evans
Linda Tellington-Jones

A special thanks to Jeannette Roach for copyediting (any existing mistakes are from my entry, not her good work), and Judy Mazer Dickerson, and Mary "Ted" Donnelly for proof reading!

And thank you,
All my two-legged and four-legged clients,
and my dearest companions and teachers,
Molly and Mitch.

Native American Legend

Once I heard a beautiful story of how dogs became man's best friend. Let me share it with you here. A long, long time ago Man wandered the Earth among all the other animals of Creation. Sadly, Man did not always act honorably toward his brothers and sisters. Creator became terribly displeased with Man's behavior and decided to separate Man from the animals. So Creator cracked open the Earth splitting Man from the animals. As the crack in the Earth widened, Man stood looking across the gap at all he had lost by treating his brothers and sisters of the animal nations poorly. The crack grew wider and wider until it was a great gorge. At the last minute, before the gulf between Man and the animals became too wide, Dog leaped across to stand beside Man. And so it is Dog chose to live in close relationship with Man as no other animal.

—Source Unknown

How To Use This Book

This book was written to be a user friendly, easy access guide to solving your dog's behavior problems. Each chapter covers one behavioral problem, and is written to stand on its own. However, please first read the introductory chapter, ***Obedience Training Is A Prerequisite For Problem Solving.*** Reading this chapter is necessary to understand the foundation for solving all behavior problems. You may then successfully proceed to the chapter appropriate to your dog's specific problem. Additionally, you may find it helpful to read the chapters, ***Health Aspects Of Behavior Problems,*** and ***Pack Psychology***.

Table of Contents

INTRODUCTION OBEDIENCE TRAINING IS A PREREQUISITE FOR PROBLEM SOLVING

Thank you for opening this book. I sincerely hope you will find it of service. This book is designed to give you easy access to clearly presented, practical instruction on resolving most canine behavioral problems. To resolve behavior problems effectively, you MUST provide your dog with a strong foundation in obedience training.

Let me say that again. Basic obedience training is a prerequisite to problem solving. When properly executed, obedience training not only gives you a basic language with which to communicate and control your dog, it builds self-control in your dog. It is that self-control within your dog that provides the foundation for problem solving. A dog that can hold a 30 minute down-stay in a distracting environment **without** reminders (repeated commands) from her owner, has enough self-control to refrain from destructive chewing when home alone or jumping on you when you return. You know that if you are self-disciplined person that quality does not stay at home when you leave for work. You will be self-disciplined at your job also. The same is true of your dog. One can build up self-discipline in one's dog through basic obedience training and then your dog can use that self-control to refrain from problem behaviors. Your dog probably already knows some of the things you do not appreciate (as I am sure you have "explained" these issues to her), but lacking self-control, she does them anyway. She can't help herself. The drive (motivation) to do the undesirable behavior wins out over her under developed self-control. Without first developing self-control within your dog, problem solving will not be successful in the long run. You may, through punishment, resolve one problem temporarily, only to have your dog act up in another way.

Some decent training manuals are listed in the back of this book. I do not agree with all the methods in any of these books (just as I do not agree with all of my own past methods), but these are some of the best. Not every method works for every trainer or each dog. You must find out what works for you as well as for your dog. In judging a training method, remember the two most important principles of dog training—consistency and NO repeated commands! In order for obedience training to be effective, your dog must be trained to respond on the first command every time. If you must call your dog three or four times before he responds, he may have already been hit by an oncoming car before he thinks to turns back to you! And if you are repeating commands (yes, this includes during correction), you are being a nagging mother soon-to-be tuned out. And you are not building self-control in your dog. A good training method will not rely on gimmicked or specialized equipment but on consistent, patient, good old fashioned hard work. That is, if you can call spending quality time with one of God's most amazing creatures work!

Speaking of time, dogs learn much faster than humans! A dog can not learn calculus but he will learn to his capacity at least twice as fast as a human. A critical learning period (how long it takes to habituate a new behavior or reshape a negative one) for a dog is about two weeks, as compared to the four week it takes a human. I guess we get to be slow because we live longer! Also Rover does not have the grocery list and upcoming work deadlines on his mind. Science now estimates the intelligence of a dog somewhere between that of a three to six year old child! You have a highly intelligent, quick, and usually very willing student. Will you take just twenty minutes a day for a few weeks to give him or her the foundation she needs to be a well-behaved and delightful pet?

There is a difference between teaching and training. Teaching is imparting comprehension of the meaning of a word or command. Training is getting your dog to obey on the first command consistently, no matter what distractions are tempting her. Many folks, either on their own or in group classes, do a good job of teaching the meaning of commands. But it is only through solid **training** that your dog will gain the necessary self-control to resolve her behavior problems.

There is also a difference between correction and punishment. Correction is an appropriate consequence of disobeying a command that has been well taught and <u>trained.</u> There are many drawbacks to punishment. Punishment is too often simply a release of the owner's frustration on the dog. When you are angrily punishing your dog, what you are saying to him is, "I am out of control. Would you like to join me?" Punishment does not teach your dog what to do right. If the punishment is too severe, your dog will be too frightened (or confused) to make the connection between his misdeed and your upset. If your dog is the least bit confused about the behavior that resulted in the punishment, he will become afraid of you and not the mistake.

Let's look at a common example. Your dog, Speedy, is racing through the house, again, after coming in from out of doors, perhaps knocking things over and otherwise creating havoc. If you bellow, "No!" Speedy will probably hit the deck. After realizing that the sky is not falling in, he'll be at it again. There is a good chance that your dog will not connect your upset and yelling with his racing through the house. And "No!" does not give Speedy anything to do right. You may just have scared the wits out of him among other things. Besides this consequence, yelling creates stress in you as well as your dog and anyone else present.

Let's reframe this scene. Suppose Speedy begins racing through the house, and you can stop the behavior by calmly putting your trained dog on a down-stay? He can make this connection, 'I was moving and now I am not.' If your dog holds the stay, you have not only ended the unwanted behavior but you get to praise him for holding the stay. A win/win situation! A positive cycle instead of a negative one of punishment. If Speedy breaks the stay, he will get a correction for a choice that he completely understands. No confusion, no stress, no fear. Over time (usually about a week) having your dog hold a down-stay whenever he comes in from out of doors will result in his coming inside calmly and laying down ON HIS OWN. Speedy will know what to do right!

Here are a few more thoughts on "No!' Usually by the time I am given a dog for private training, the dog thought his first and last name are "No!" "No!Rover!No!" He had learned to ignore "no" and his other name, as well! When "no' is properly taught and trained, it is spoken in a normal tone and volume (not a loud, harsh voice) and means to stop whatever you are doing immediately. Therefore, "no" has limited use and needs to be followed by some direction on what to do. A good example of an appropriate use of "no" is that of a very young pup caught chewing something it should not. "No" means cease and desist…stop whatever you are doing immediately. "No" should be followed by trading the forbidden object with a proper chew toy. It is much more productive to give your dog a positive command to obey than to rely on "no" to stop problem behaviors. "No" is only a temporary fix, at best.

Now that I have said my piece on the absolute necessity of good, solid obedience training that builds self-control as a prerequisite to problem solving, let us move on and look at some of the less obvious effects of obedience training as it pertains to problem solving. Proper obedience training indirectly resolves many behavior problems because it is the most direct way one can correct the pack order in your home, placing the two leggeds above the four. One does not enter his or her boss' office uninvited, prop one's feet up on the boss' desk, use his or her stationary for personal business and eat the boss' lunch! Similarly, dogs do not invade a pack leader's domain, jumping up, mouthing and chewing the leader's toys and stealing her food. I was often asked, when meeting a client's dog for the first time, why their dog did not jump on me, mouth my hands or otherwise molest me when it did everyone else? It is simply that dogs recognize me as a leader not an equal or underling. Underlying many folks' reluctance to assert dominance over their dog is the fear that their dogs will not love them if they are boss. This fear is most certainly unfounded. Dogs embody loyalty. You can have love and respect from your dog. Remember, a pack with its pecking order is the natural social order for dogs. Having a strong, benevolent leader imparts a feeling of security and well being, allowing an even closer bond between dog and human.

Another benefit of obedience training is that it facilitates the socialization of your dog to any number of situations. A dog must be well socialized with humans (at home and in public), with other animals, and she must be desensitized to a variety of places, sights, and sounds to be a well-adjusted pet in our society. If you have gained control of your dog through basic training, you can successfully take your dog out in public to meet people; you can prevent or resolve shyness problems; provide your dog with opportunities to play with other animals, preventing dog aggression and predatory behaviors (besides having fun). You can desensitize your dog to new sights and sounds, preventing situational shyness. Not only will a sit-stay make your dog more inviting to meet, but it will give your dog the self confidence not to be frightened by strangers approaching. That sit-stay will provide her with the self-control necessary to reject the temptation to lunge or growl aggressively. The bond of leadership and sense of security created through training allows your dog to explore new situations. This is a self-perpetuating positive cycle of spending more and more quality time with you, to your enjoyment as well as your canine companion's. Your dog will be a delight to be around enhancing your life as well as his own. What a difference from the limited life that the burden of a poorly behaved dog suffers!

HEALTH ASPECTS OF BEHAVIOR PROBLEMS:

How diet and exercise affect behavior.

General good health produces a feeling of well being that enhances anyone's right actions. The same is true of your canine companion. If your dog feels well physically, he or she will be better able to learn what you desire and better behaved in general.

Of course, the foundation of good health is proper diet and exercise. A good quality dry dog food, that's main source of protein (first ingredient on the label) is meat, is essential. I do not believe that soybeans are a highly digestible quality source of protein for a carnivore. I do believe that soy-based ingredients contribute to flatulence and possibly bloat. High protein (above 22%) dog foods are not desirable. High protein may cause young dogs to grow too fast and possibly become overweight, interfering with the proper formation of joints. This may increase the possibility of clinical hip and elbow displasia (as well as other health problems). If your joints hurt, you are unable to move freely. Pain may make your dog grouchy and unable to concentrate and to learn. Secondly, feeding high protein is like feeding your dog jet fuel when he only needs regular gasoline.

High-protein levels may contribute to hyperactivity. Finally, excess protein is cleared through the kidneys. Why cause your puppy to have to urinate more frequently than necessary, especially during house training?

I look for a dog food that is naturally preserved and contains no dyes, and no artificial flavorings. There is some reason to believe that these chemicals may contribute to disease in the long term and hyperactivity in the short term. If possible, avoid foods that contain byproducts. The ingredient "chicken byproducts", for example, includes beaks, feathers and feet as well as other even less desirable parts.

Aerobic exercise is the second component of a healthy lifestyle for your dog. Medium to large dogs should get at least a one mile (15–20 minute) aerobic walk daily. Small dogs should get at least a half mile (10 minute) aerobic walk daily. By aerobic, I mean no stopping. If most humans walk briskly, most dogs will trot. Not only does aerobic exercise add vitality to the body but it causes the release of endorphins in the brain producing a relaxed feeling of well being. Aerobic exercise also helps burn off excess energy. A relaxed, tired dog is a well behaved dog! Do not jog with a dog under two years of age. Growth plates in the long bones should be fused before the pounding that jogging may entail. Let your dog eliminate before starting your aerobic walk. Your dog can relax and sniff afterwards.

No, just being outside in the yard does not count in the exercise department. It is a rare dog (just like it is a rare human) that will sufficiently exercise without some external motivation. No, a game of fetch will not replace the aerobic walk either unless your dog is chasing that ball non stop for 15 minutes. Keep playing ball and letting Rover hang out in the yard, but add the aerobic walk into your daily routine also.

If your dog is overweight, put him on a diet! Being fat is uncomfortable, makes one grouchy and less able to learn well. Obesity also contributes to skin problems which add another layer of discomfort. Please, if your dog has skin problems, do not use steroids to treat them except as an absolute last resort. I have seen prednisolone and other steroid therapies cause aggression in dogs.

In my opinion, spaying and neutering is a moral responsibility of every pet owner. There are literally millions of unwanted dogs put to death every year, many of which are purebreds. If done properly there is no money in breeding. Beyond the ethics of spaying and neutering, there are the positive behavioral benefits as well. Spayed females don't have PMS, which can drastically change disposition. Yes, dogs experience disposition changes during hormone fluctuations just as humans do. Males are more tractable, less likely to roam and mark territory (ruining both your landscaping, and your neighbor's as well) when neutered. There are also some life threatening health problems that spaying and neutering may help avoid, such as breast cancer, pyrometria and prostitis. Spaying or neutering will not make your dog fat. Eating too much and not getting enough exercise cause obesity. It is estimated that as much as one third of all the calories taken in by an intact dog are used by the reproductive tract. So after spaying or neutering, feed your dog accordingly.

In addition to a healthy diet and proper exercise, a comprehensive vaccination and parasite prevention program are required for optimum health. If your dog has a tummy ache from worms or itches from fleas he will not be able to concentrate well on his lessons. Your veterinarian can outline these programs for you.

There are some physical problems that may directly cause behavior problems. One is deafness. Obviously, if your dog does not have good hearing he is going to be harder to communicate with. Deafness is most often associated with the black and white color pattern of Dalmatians and Harlequin Great Danes, but it can occur in any breed or mix. Unfortunately, owners often mistake deafness for stubbornness or lack of intelligence. Microopthalmia (small eyes) and other vision problems also will interfere with how your dog reacts in certain situations and how he or she learns. Dogs with vision problems often exhibit fearful, flighty or shy behaviors such as barking in panic at newly positioned or unusual objects in their environment or apparent fear of doorways and stairs. Rage Syndrome is an unusual form of epilepsy in which the afflicted dog goes into aggressive behaviors instead of seizures when his brain short circuits. Rage Syndrome varies in severity and is most common in show bloodlines of male English Springer Spaniels, although it does occur in other breeds and mixes. There are some other health-based issues that I will cover under specific problems such as the role of mineral deficiency in chewing problems and pancreatitis in aggression.

PACK PSYCHOLOGY

Dogs are pack animals. If not in a wild dog pack, then, a dog's pack is formed by other animals, most often the humans with which he lives. This mixed pack, human/dog/cat is the situation with which we are concerned. However, a look at the wild dog pack or its ancestor, the wolf pack, will shed light on our present situation.

Every pack has an order of dominance (a pecking order), from the leader down to the most inferior underling or follower. For a dog to be a well-adjusted, mannerly, happy pet, she must be lower than all humans in order of dominance in the mixed pack. It is the dog's confusion or misperception (perhaps the human is too) about her position in respect to the humans that is the root of most behavioral problems. Being a follower relieves stress and creates a sense of security.

This survival of the pack depends on strong leadership. The alpha, top dog, must be brave, intelligent, and physically strong to successfully lead his or her pack on the hunt. The collective results of a pack's hunts determine whether it will flourish or starve. It is necessary for the underlings to challenge the leader occasionally to make sure that he or she is not faltering. If the challenge is properly put down, order will be restored. The leader will not harbor ill feelings toward the challenging underling because it is not an emotional issue, although often interpreted as such by humans. Such challenges are a normal test for survival. If the challenge is not completely suppressed, it is the directive of nature to further test the leadership. Eventually the testing follower will assume the leadership position.

Looking at an example in the mixed human/dog pack, the naturally pushy puppy that growls over her food bowl and is not properly corrected is one step toward alpha. Her human may believe the old wives tale that one must not bother a dog when it is eating. But in the pup's mind she just said, "Back off!" and won. Another, more subtle example, is the "retrieving human." You know the game and so does Princess. Human throws the ball, dog does not get it, so human does. Who's the boss? What about pulling on the leash, and chase games?

The confusion in pack order is usually a result of humans not understanding or speaking "Dog." Dogs have highly evolved means of communication involving eye contact, body posture and some sounds. Since your dog cannot learn to use English in the same manner you do, you must learn how to speak "Dog."

Body posture is one of the primary means by which the boss dog communicates with his or her pack. Does your little John Wayne walk around all puffed up on his toes, hackles up, ears erect, tail up, as if he owns the place? Or is your dog the Dagwood type, with ears laid back, body lowered, tail down and wagging when he approaches you. What does your body posture say to your dog?

Another important aspect of dog language is eye contact. The strong leader can just look at an underling, causing the follower to cower and avert his or her eyes. Sound anything like bowing to royalty? If your dog defiantly refuses to meet your eye, she is saying you do not exist, you are not worthy. You can teach good eye contact by sitting your dog facing you and saying, "Look at me when I talk to you" as you trace a line from your dog's eye to your eye. Do this when no other pack members are present. At first you may have to take a hold of Butch's muzzle and force him to look at you. The split second he does, look away and release him. This takes 5 seconds or less. Do it twice a day.

Dogs also communicate through sound. Puppies whine to express anxiety, "I'm cold, hungry or my pillow needs fluffing." Dogs bark in excitement to warn away intruders or when playing. All these barks sound different to the educated ear. When I moved to Delaware, I even deciphered a "There's a snake in my kennel," bark! Growls have various meanings also—some playful, some threatening. Body posture often determines the meaning of similar sounds. Finally there is the howl used in a pack sing along or when one member is lonely or mourning.

Studies have been done graphing the sounds dogs make and human speech patterns. The graph of the pleading dog owner, "Please, p–l–e–a–s–e be a good little snooky ookums," looks a lot like a whining pup on a graph. The pleading owner's puppy cannot understand most of the words but understands the inflection. The goodbye lecture given by some dog owners when preparing to leave their dog home alone, says to the pup, "You have good reason to be upset." Then there is the over domineering human that is constantly barking, "No! No! No!" all day and wonders why the pup urinates when he or she approaches. This owner is often at a loss for the cause of their dog's shy, submissive behaviors claiming, "But, I've never even smacked Wimpy once!"

It is important to remember to use correct voice inflection when giving commands to your dog. Do not shout or sound harsh—just firm. Shouting or a harsh tone creates tension in you and your dog. However, do not ask questions by raising the pitch of your voice at the end of the word. This can communicate anxiety like a whine. Besides, you are the boss. Give commands, don't make requests!

The final, and most important element of verbal communication with your dog, is silence! The wild dog pack communicates mostly through eye contact and body posture. If they ran around the woods barking all day, they would scare away the prey on which they depend! Even worse than barking is to hear a constant babble of unintelligible English from your human pack member. Nag, nag, nag—remember how you could tune out your mother? So zip your lips and that tuned-out adolescent canine may just start looking to you to see what's up?

OK, now that you have the basics, let us look at some common situations that give your dog an over-inflated opinion of his or her pack position. Leaders lead through doorways, gates and upstairs. Allowing Flash to rush in and out the main entrances of your territory, your house and yard, tells him that he is the LEADER! It may not be a big deal to you, but it is to your dog. Besides, it is dangerous. A door bolting dog can easily trip an unsuspecting person or dash out into traffic. To cure door bolting, have Flash hold a sit-stay as you open the door. If your dog breaks the stay, shut the door and correct. Practice until you can open and shut the door, go in and out, even go out and shut the door, while your dog waits patiently for permission to pass (release command). Then have Flash sit on the other side of the door waiting for your next command, instead of rushing off to play in the traffic. "Courtesy at the door" also helps resolve those mad scenes when company arrives.

Teach your dog the word "Scoot". Which means just that, "I'm pack leader, make way!" When your dog has parked herself in the geographical center of the room disrupting the flow of traffic, tell her to, "Scoot!" and guide her to the side lines by the collar. Do not walk around her. That communicates deference on your part. Also make her move if she is parked in a doorway you wish to go through or in front of the couch where you want to sit.

Another subtle way in which the pack order is confused is feeding dogs human food. In the wild pack, the leader eats the best parts of a kill first, then the other pack members eat the leftovers. Translation into the human/dog pack is, humans eat human food and dogs eat dog food.

Following this same logic, the wild pack leader chooses the best place to sleep, and the followers then pick a spot at a respectful distance. Translation—humans sleep in beds, dogs sleep on the floor. Besides, not allowing your dog to sleep in your bed keeps it clean and flea free.

Picture, if you will, the wife of the traveling salesman. Hubby is out of town frequently. That is one of the main reasons they got Killer. Now having Killer fill the empty spot in the bed, makes the Mrs. feel more secure. Of course, Killer gets the message, "I'm in charge and have to protect my subordinates." So when Hubby returns home and orders Killer off the bed, Killer's bite is just a proper suppression of a challenge to his alpha position.

Tug-o-war and extreme roughhousing teaches the dog to vie for control with their humans by using their mouth. In tug-o-war, you are teaching your dog to growl, bite, and clamp down to gain possession of an object—heaven forbid if it is an old sock! Not only are you teaching "Rowdy" to use his mouth against you, you have lowered yourself to his level! Roughhousing also teaches your dog to be aggressive with humans. Later, when you want to calmly scratch Rowdy's ear, are you annoyed when he mouths your hand to initiate a game? It is unrealistic and unfair to teach a behavior in one situation and not expect it to be generalized.

The best game to play with your dog is fetch. If she will not bring the ball back, put her on the leash so you can gently guide her in. Keep it light and fun. If your dog refuses to release the toy, place your hand on the muzzle, thumb on one side, fore finger on the other and squeeze her lips in between the teeth of her upper and lower jaws. Say, "Give," as you do this. If your dog does not retrieve, do not retrieve for her! Who's in charge of whom if you repeatedly run out to get the ball? My Molly's opinion of the game of ball is, "If you want the dumb ball, don't throw it away in the first place!"

Many dogs get a spoiled brat attitude of, "Here I am, come love wonderful me," because their owners lavish unearned attention on them constantly. This is understandable since we usually get pups to love, and their cute little faces are so inviting. However, if you place no demands on your pup as he grows, you will create a monster. A canine mother cares for her infant pup's every need. But, as that pup matures, he has rules and responsibilities placed upon him.

Most petting should be the result of your dog correctly responding to your wishes. All petting must be earned if you are trying to reform a canine hoodlum. The sit in front is the best way to start having your pup earn attention. It is also the best way to end a jumping problem. EVERY time Gigolo approaches you or you go to him, have him sit before you pet him. This includes when he nudges you for a pat while you are watching TV. Pet Gigolo briefly (a few seconds) and stop, or give him another command so you can pet him some more.

By now I hope you have concluded that obedience training is a prerequisite to raising a mannerly pup or reforming the canine hoodlum. Basic obedience training is the most direct means of establishing your dominance. It provides a basic language for communication, and if done properly, builds self control in your dog. Practical obedience training provides the bases for the resolution of many problems through, "courtesy at the door," the "sit-in-front," and the down-stay, just to mention a few. Additionally, an occasional surprise, "Down," clearly says to your dog, "I am the boss and don't you forget it!" Also one long down-stay a day (build up to at least 30 minutes), builds the kind of self control your dog needs to refrain from problem behaviors. Self control is not a different quality for different situations. If you are self disciplined at home, you can apply that ability at work.

Similarly, if your dog has enough self control to hold a 30 minute down-stay around heavy distraction, she has enough self control to refrain from jumping on people, rushing doors, and so forth.

You can create a special form of praise by singing to your dog. Pick an up beat tune and mix your pup's name and nick names into the lyrics. Sing Maestro's little ditty when he behaves especially well or needs a pick me up. My dear old lady, Molly, would turn herself inside out for Winnie the Pooh with her name in it!

Some of the things I have suggested seem harsh. Often owners fear that if they correct their dogs, then their dogs will not love them any more. The opposite is true. Dogs are drawn to strong leaders—it is their nature. A strong leader makes them feel secure. You can have love and respect by balancing praise and petting with discipline and guidance. Good Luck, Boss!!

STARTING YOUR NEW PUP OFF ON THE RIGHT PAW

Wow! What a privilege, a new dog! A pet is a privilege, not a right. A pet is also a responsibility. Be sure you are prepared to meet a pet's physical and emotional needs. With just a little forethought and planning, introducing a new dog into your home can go smoothly. Starting your puppy off on the right paw, is much easier than correcting problems you have created. Raising a pup to be a well-adjusted, mannerly adult may be one of the most rewarding endeavors of your life. A pet's purpose is to enhance our lives with the unique joy that only she can provide. It is not to be a burden that an untrained, disobedient dog too often becomes. A little doggie sense (that's common sense from your dog's point of view) and an eye to the future will get you and your pup started off on the right paw.

If you have not selected your puppy yet, here are a few words to the wise. Choose a breed or mixed breed of dog based on his personality, not appearance. Please use the breed counseling questionnaire to prevent a mismatch between you and your future dog. Buy your pup form a reputable breeder. A breeder is a person actively involved in the improvement his or her breed. A reputable breeder will also guarantee his pups beyond 48 hours. Ideally the guarantee will cover temperament as well as physical problems.

Pick your puppy up when she is seven weeks old where the law allows. Do not pick up your pup prior to seven weeks of age. There are important lessons best taught in the litter in the first seven weeks, such as how hard and often mouthing is acceptable. The next best age for optimum adjustment is nine weeks. Never pick your pup up during the eighth week of age. It is a critical fear imprint week. The trauma of being removed from one's litter mates and mom during the eighth week could permanently scar your pup's temperament resulting in shyness.

Have your pup vetted within a few days and follow your veterinarian's program for vaccination and deworming (wormy pups are difficult to housebreak).

One more preliminary. If everyone in your household is gone during the day, seriously consider getting an older dog. It is unfair to a young pup to try to raise it in a working household. Older dogs adjust beautifully and become adoring companions. If you already have a young pup in a working household, you will have to make some special efforts to be fair to your pup and realize that training is going to take twice as long.

In order to enhance health and housetraining, your puppy should be fed a high quality meat-based dry dog that is naturally preserved. Ideally the food should not contain any soybean (a cheap, indigestible source of protein), dyes, byproducts or sugar. I do **NOT** recommend puppy formulas except in special situations. 22% protein is good for most dogs and puppies. The high protein levels of puppy formulas can cause increased urination (excess protein is cleared from the body through the kidneys), hyperactivity, and overweight, which can increase the likelihood of the development of clinical hip and elbow displasia, and skin problems, among other things.

Housetraining, teaching your pup to eliminate outside, cannot formally begin until a pup is 10–12 weeks old. If crate training is attempted when the pup is too young, it may not have the physical capacity to keep the crate clean. Having to stay in a dirty crate may destroy a pup's instinct to keep its den clean and make housetraining difficult or impossible. Until your pup is old enough to begin crate training, confine the pup to a small room with the floor completely covered with newspaper, and walk your pup outside on a regular basis.

When the pup begins to show some physical control (usually 10–12 weeks), confine it to a crate both at night and when you cannot keep an eye on it. The crate takes advantage of the dog's natural instinct to keep its den clean. Dogs do not dislike their crates unless you use them for punishment or isolation.

Walk your pup first thing in the morning, and about every 1–2 hours throughout the day, also walk the pup after meals, playtime, other periods of excitement (company arriving, departing, etc.), and last thing at night. Confine your pup for 10 minutes prior to every potty walk. Only allow your pup 3–5 minutes for a potty walk or she may forget why she's outside. If your pup completely eliminates, reward with supervised freedom in the house for 1–2 hours. If your pup does not completely eliminate, confine it to its crate for 15 minutes and walk it again. Accidents should be few if humans follow this program. The occasional mistake should be cleaned up with club soda on carpet and white vinegar on hard surfaces. Do not rub your pup's nose in accidents or beat the pup!!! As your pup grows and develops more bowel and bladder control, you can increase the length of time between potty walks. At six to eight months of age, most pups develop complete bowel and bladder control. Now you can begin gradually weaning your pup out of the crate gradually or begin expanding the space your pup has access to if you are paper training.

Excessive destructive chewing is unfortunately taught to most pups by humans. Don't overwhelm your pup with toys or shove something in it's mouth every time you want to pacify it. Chewing toys should have two qualities. They should not be confusing and they should be indestructible. Do not give your pup rawhide chewies if you do not want them to chew your shoes and other leather. Do not give your pup old socks with knots tied in them if you do not want her to chew other fabric. Acceptable toys are Nylabones or the softer puppy version, Gumabones, a solid rubber ball or a "Natural Bone" (purchased at pet shops, these are real bones that have been treated so they will not splinter). By following the aforementioned housetraining program, your pup will have few opportunities for destructive chewing during the teething stage since it will be supervised, outside or in its crate. Grannick's Bitter Apple may be used to discourage your pup form chewing the wrong things. Bitter Apple is extract of sour apples in an alcohol base. Apply it when your pup is not present to effect a cure. Otherwise, she will not chew when she sees you spray things but will merrily chew away when objects are left untreated. DO NOT punish your pup for chewing. Punishment often feeds the problem because dogs often chew when bored or lonely.

Negative attention (punishment) is better than no attention to many pups.

Dogs jump to get attention and to give affection. Resist the urge to pet your pup when she jumps up. It teaches a behavior that will not be so cute when your pup is an adult. Instead gently place your pup in a sit every time she approaches you or you approach her. This teaches your pup to politely ask, "Pet me please?" instead of demanding your attention by jumping. The sit-in-front also develops a positive attitude of having your pup looking for ways to please you and earn attention, rather than a spoiled brat demanding a lot of attention for doing nothing.

Do not feed your pup from the table if you do not want a little beggar. Little pups should not be given human food because it may upset the bowels causing housetraining problems. Feed your pup only from her bowl. Do not allow your dog to lick plates on the floor if you do not want her to lick them on the table. Giving dogs human food can also contribute to dominance problems. As we've discussed, in the wild, the pack leader gets the choice food and the rest of the pack get the leftovers. The translation of this law into the human household is, dogs eat dog food, humans eat human food.

Do not allow little pups to sit on your lap when you are sitting on the furniture if you do not want your adult dog to get on the furniture. If you do not mind your dog taking over your furniture, that is up to you. However, such freedom can cause confusion in the pack order. Pack leaders get the best places to sleep. Translation is humans on the furniture and dogs on the floor. Also think about the dirt an adult dog may track on the furniture.

Mouthing, grabbing, and biting your hands and legs, is a normal puppy behavior that can get out of hand. Do not play slap-around-the-face games with your puppy. And worse yet is tug-o-war. These games can cause severe mouthing problems and much worse, aggression problems. The best game to teach your pup is fetch. Fetch teaches your pup to <u>come</u> to you and the reward (your throwing the toy again) is built into the game.

Start teaching your pup to accept grooming and examination of her feet, ears, and teeth at an early age. Your veterinarian will appreciate it and your dog will get better health care.

Do not call your pup and then punish her or do anything she

considers unpleasant (such as bathing, putting in a crate, etc.) This will teach your pup <u>NOT</u> to come when called. Go get your pup in these situations. Always have coming to you mean a pleasant reward of praise (<u>occasionally</u> a food treat).

Basic obedience training is a must for every dog to be a truly enjoyable companion. Training establishes a basic language in which you and your dog can communicate. Perhaps more importantly, training develops self-control in your dog and it also prevents or resolves most canine behavior problems. I recommend training under the guidance of a qualified professional. Group classes provide some socialization (class alone is not sufficient socialization). Private instruction is more successful than a group because you get individualized attention and it moves at your pace. Well-taught classes and private lessons should include basic obedience training <u>and</u> lectures on typical problems such as housetraining, chewing, etc. Boarding school is the most successful training program because all you have to do is learn how to handle a professionally trained dog. This form of training has many advantages for folks with busy schedules, handicaps or difficult dogs, among other things. If such guidance is not available in your area, get a copy of <u>The Koehler Method of Dog Training</u> by William Koehler (published by Howell) and follow it to the letter (with the exception of the hole digging correction which I do not recommend). Puppies can begin training at four months of age (*teaching* can begin as soon as you get your pup).

This chapter is just meant as a primer to get your pup started on the right paw. Please read on, especially the chapters on housetraining, chewing, and jumping!

INTRODUCING AN OLDER PUP OR DOG INTO YOUR HOME

Bless you if you plan to adopt one of the millions of homeless older dogs. Making a responsible choice is your duty to yourself, your family and the dog! There are a few special considerations when selecting an older pup or dog. It should go with out saying that the adoptee should have been raised with children if you have kids. Also, consider the new dog's history with other animals if you have cats or livestock. Get as much background information as you can on your secondhand dog, including a medical history, behavior problems, and former living situations. If you tell the former owners that you are sending the dog to training school, they are often more forthcoming in identifying the misbehaviors of your future pet. When adopting an older dog, you should get it on a thirty-day trial basis. Often dogs are changing homes for problems that may not be disclosed by the former owner or are unknown to an adoption organization. Have your new dog thoroughly vetted shortly after you get it to ferret out any health problems. Time will tell if you can manage other problems that present themselves or if you would be better off adopting a different dog. It is also in the best interest of the dog that you keep him no longer than thirty days if you uncover major problems, but give him a fair trial of at least a couple of weeks.

When clients have consulted me prior to picking up a new dog, I have explained two schools of thought about when to begin training. The first is to bring the dog straight from its former home to boarding school. Training provides basic control of the dog and self-control in the dog, the foundation for preventing and resolving behavior problems. Training prior to the dog's entering a client home allows me to work on any known problems before the dog could establish the behaviors in his new home. The other school of thought is for the new owner to have the dog in his or her home for one month before sending it to training. This allowed the client time to get to know the dog and make sure it was one that he or she would like to keep. By having the new dog for one month, the dog had a chance to adjust to the change of homes before the stress of school and not too very long to get set in bad ways in its new home. For the dog's sake, the first option is best. For the new owner's pocketbook, perhaps, the second was the safest.

Preventing problems in your home is far superior to trying to resolve them once they start. Treat your new dog as though he or she is an unhousetrained puppy whether or not he was supposed to have been housetrained in his former home. Even the best house trained dogs may have an accident under the stress of changing homes. So confine your new dog to a cage when home alone or you cannot supervise him. Otherwise, put your new dog outside in a securely fenced, topped, and bottomed kennel. In spite of what you may have been told about the dog, you do not know if this dog will jump a fence or dig out in an unfamiliar environment. To prevent stomach upset and the possible resulting housetraining accidents, for the first week, feed your new dog whatever he was eating in his former home. If the diet is not of good quality, after the first week, gradually switch your new dog over to a better food. If your new dog is over eight months old, potty walk it every four hours. If your new dog is under eight months treat it as unhousetrained puppy (see the chapter on housetraining). If there are no accidents after a couple of weeks, you can start to give you new dog more freedom and responsibility.

By closely supervising your new dog and confining it when you cannot, you will also prevent destructive chewing that may occur do to the stress of changing homes. Right from the very start, do not allow any behaviors from your new dog that you do not wish to be permanent in her repertoire...no jumping on you, climbing on the furniture, begging, roughhousing, etc.

Walk your new dog on leash for two weeks, <u>at the very least!</u> Even if she was off-leash controllable in her former home, the dog needs <u>at least</u> two weeks for a bond to begin to form with you. If you know that the dog was not off leash trained before you got her, do not let her off leash until you have her trained! Running away is a very common reason dogs wind up for adoption, so assume the worst and be careful! Remember our earlier admonition not to call your dog and then punish her or do anything she considers unpleasant (such as bathing, confining to a crate, etc.) Your new friend will quickly learn that <u>"coming"</u> often has unpleasant results. Go get your dog in these situations. Always have coming to you mean a reward of praise and <u>occasionally</u> a food treat.

OK, you have gotten your new dog off on the right paw and have committed to keeping her. Go to School! Ideally you receive instruction from the former owner in your adoptee's training but that is a rare situation. Even if your new dog was trained prior to your adopting her, you need to learn to speak a common language. Not all training methods are the same. Basic obedience training is a must for every dog to be a truly enjoyable companion. Good luck and enjoy your new best friend!

INTRODUCING A SECOND DOG INTO YOUR HOME

Besotted with the love and fun of a dog, one often thinks a second dog will be twice the affection and joy. I know how much a dog can bring into your life but more than one dog usually does NOT mean twice the pleasure! In most situations one dog is ideal, both for the dog and the humans. So let's have a few sobering words here about multi-dog ownership. Very few families in today's busy world truly have time to accommodate the needs of more than one pet. We just have a limited amount of time and energy. Two dogs require more than twice as much effort than one. Usually one dog becomes the other dog's dog and is not primarily bonded to the humans. Not only does this mean that the full enjoyment of the human-dog relationship is not available to the owners, but it decreases the control the owner has over both dogs! The dominant dog is less likely to listen to a human because he or she has a dog to lead and the underling is going to respond primarily to the dominant dog, and not the human. DO NOT get a second dog because you feel guilty about not spending enough time with you first dog! Either give your present dog more time or find her a home where her emotional as well as her physical needs will be met.

A single dog forms his pack with the humans in the home, a mixed pack. Two dogs, depending on the temperament and age each was acquired, may be more bonded to each other and less bonded to the humans in the household. With three or more dogs in one home, the dogs will begin to form a true dog pack, exclusive of the humans present. A pack greatly changes the behavior of your dogs. A pack will do things that an individual dog would not. If the pack members are not well balanced, some dog is going to be the odd "man" out. The others may gang up on him. The resulting dog fights are potentially disastrous. Not only may the dogs be injured or worse, but humans often get bitten trying to break up fights. There is also emotional damage done to four leggeds as well as the two leggeds when the solution becomes to get rid of one or more of the dogs. Very often children suffer in this situation. Not only is there the potential for a serious physical injury, but there is the possibility of heartbreak if children are asked to part with a beloved friend. So DO NOT set yourself, your family, or any innocent dogs up in this potential misfortune.

If you are committed to having a second dog, select her carefully. Please use the breed counseling questionnaire to prevent a mismatch between you and your new dog. DO NOT get a second dog until your first is at least two years(age of mental maturity in dogs) and well behaved. One dog will teach another faster than a human. Your well-behaved dog can positively influence the second. A poorly behaved dog can teach the new dog all her bad habits!

Even if your present dog is spayed or neutered and the new one is or will shortly be altered, get opposite sexes. They are the least likely to fight. The second best combination is two females. Though two males often cohabit with out problems, it is just as frequent that they cannot. Once again, do not set yourself up needlessly for the heartbreak of having to place one of the dogs in another home after you, and your family, and the dogs are attached to one another!

Both dogs should be dogs that have been well socialized around other dogs all their lives with no history of dog aggression. It should go without saying that the adoptee should have been raised with children if you have kids. Also, consider the new dog's history with other animals if you have cats or livestock. Making a responsible choice is your duty to yourself, your family and the dog!

Before bringing your new dog home, pick up all dog toys, food bowls, and beds so there are no "bones of contention" to the dogs to fight over. First impressions are often lasting ones. Introduce your new dog and your original dog on neutral territory, NOT in your home or yard, or in the former residence of the new dog. A local park will do. Have one handler for each dog. Introduce them on leash. DO NOT hold the leashes taut when introducing the dogs!!! The pain in the neck each dog feels will be associated with the other dog. You can pull the dogs apart should they fight just as quickly if you have allowed one inch (enough to relieve pressure on the neck) of slack in the leash as you can if the leash is taut. If the dogs seem to be getting on OK, take them to your home in separate automobiles or crate the new dog. You do not want a fight breaking out in the car while you are driving. Your car is your present dog's territory! Once on your property, introduce the dogs again outdoors and thoroughly potty walk both to prevent marking in your house. Again, be cautious when taking them inside, because the new dog is now invading your first dog's den. Allow both dogs to trail leashes around inside so you can safely separate them should a battle erupt. Feed the dogs separately or closely supervised at opposite ends of a room until they are well adjusted to each other and have learned to eat from their own bowls only. If all is well (absolutely no aggression between the dogs), after a couple of weeks, you can try giving the dogs toys and beds. Supervise the dogs whenever they have toys to play with for at least two more weeks.

Sound like a lot of trouble for a situation that will probably go well? It is a lot less trouble than trying to reintroduce dogs once they have gotten off to a bad start or taking an injured dog or two, or worse, a bitten human, to the hospital! Play it safe.

AGGRESSION TOWARD HUMANS

Aggression toward humans is the most serious and dangerous of canine sins, the cardinal of which is aggression toward his owner and family! I strongly recommend that you seek professional help from a trainer qualified to handle aggressive dogs if you are experiencing an aggression problem with your pet. The worst thing you can do is deny the problem or make excuses for aggressive behavior. "Max only growls over his food." "It's because he was an abused puppy." "German Shepherds are supposed to be protective!" All of these statements may be true and all are varying levels of denial and excuses for what may be the beginning of the most serious of problems. Indulging in excuses may lose valuable time. There is a point of no return in some situations!

Let us look at each of these statements closely. German Shepherds, Doberman Pinschers, Rottweilers and many other breeds were bred to be guard dogs of various sorts. That is exactly why they may not be a good choice as a pet in many situations. Even in homes and businesses that have a legitimate need for protection, the person choosing a dog of a guard breed must be willing to accept the responsibility of managing such an animal. If a person is not willing to be a strong, dominant pack leader and responsibly handle a guard dog, a security system and a Sheltie may be a better choice. What does "properly managing" a guard breed dog mean exactly? It means thorough socialization, and strict obedience training, things such as requiring visitors to knock and wait before being invited into your home (even relatives, close neighbors and friends). Also, a guard breed must never be allowed to run at large in a neighborhood. *A guard breed must never be chained up outdoors!* Chaining may cause uncontrollable aggression problems (and barking and digging). Seriously consider the need for a fenced area, even if you plan to walk your dog on a leash. There may be times, due to illness or injury, when you are unable to walk your dog.

Ninety-five percent or more of aggressive behaviors are rooted in shyness. Shyness is the most prevalent temperament problem. Genetically, shyness is the flip side of forward aggression. Therefore, there are great deal of shy dogs within the guard breeds as well as the general dog population. Shyness is the stable protectiveness so valued in German Shepherd Dogs and other guard breeds gone bad. Although a shy dog may appear forward aggressive, the source of the behavior is fear. Hence, the name fear biter. How does the behavior progress from backing away to apparent forward aggression?

First, a little background in wild dog pack development. Sometime during the "teenage stage" (6–9 months) of development, Bully is out in the yard alone. He has recently discovered his voice (this is the age dogs really start to bark in earnest) and is testing it out on anything that moves. Although Bully may appear adult in size, at this age he is still a pup at heart and in mind. If he were in a wild pack, his parents, aunts, and uncles would be leaving him and his litter mates home alone a little longer while the pack is out hunting. This is a natural time to begin asserting independence. These wild pups would now wander a little farther from their den. Although near-adult in size, these adolescents lack the skill to fight to defend themselves. So Mother Nature builds in a greater tendency toward flight at this age. Hence, the name "flight stage." This is the age when most pups stop coming when called and start running away.

Back to Bully in the yard. He is barking at every passerby and backing away in retreat as he does. But one day, the passerby, too often a child, is startled by Bully's verbal onslaught and retreats before Bully does. The light bulb flashes on in Bully's head, "Hey! Lookie what I can do. I can scare them more than they scare me!" The true Bully now finds delight in this new game. If not counterbalanced with proper training and socialization under the direction of a strong pack leader, the snowball has started rolling down the hill to a bad end…the forward aggressive acting dog.

Examining a little more wolf pack psychology will shed light on many aggression problems. Being highly social animals that live in groups, wolves and dogs have a definite "pecking" or pack social order. Packs are not run on the consensus model. A pack would not survive long in the wild if decisions had to be made by committee. An intelligent, strong, dominant leader must be in charge for the pack to be successful on the hunt and to keep peace among its members. Because survival of the pack is dependent on strong leadership, Mother Nature requires underlings to challenge leadership occasionally. These tests are necessary to expose weaknesses that might be detrimental to the pack's well being. If these challenges are properly put down, peace is restored. On the other hand, if such challenges are ignored or insufficiently handled, then the challenging underling as well as other pack members are compelled to test again. This is not malicious, but Nature's way of ensuring that leadership is strong and that only the most sound reproduce. (In wolf pack, usually only the alpha male and his female reproduce, unless food is very plentiful; in that case the beta pair may also mate.)

Our pets obviously do not live in wild packs, but they do live in a group that represents that pack. Their mixed pack consists of you, your dog(s) and the other humans and animals who live in your household. As it is the nature of your dog to assume leadership if you do not, you must be a strong yet benevolent leader from the time your pet enters your pack to prevent aggression and other behavior problems.

Inappropriate play can contribute to aggressive behavior. Some breeds, Rottweilers in particular, must never be engaged in games of tug-o-war or roughhousing. Tug-o-war teaches your dog to vie for control of an object with their humans, supposedly pack leaders, by using their mouth. When tugging with your dog, you are teaching him to growl, bite, and clamp down! Sound like aggressive behavior to you? Not only are you teaching your dog to use his mouth against you, you have lowered yourself to his level in the pack! Roughhousing may also teach your dog to behave aggressively toward humans. Later, when you want to calmly scratch your dog's ear, you are annoyed when he mouths your hand to initiate a game. It is unrealistic and unfair to teach a behavior in one situation and not expect it to be generalized.

Perhaps the most disheartening cause of canine aggression is human aggression. Violence incenses violence. If you have been beating your dog, STOP IT! You are teaching him to be aggressive by your own nasty, cruel behavior. If you terrify your dog with a spanking, not only are you be teaching him aggression but you are most likely failing to correct the problem you are punishing him for. If a punishment is too frightening, the terrified dog will stop thinking and failing to make the connection between his misdeed and your angry abuse. Your dog is learning to fear you and fight aggressively to defend himself.

Another possible source of aggression is a health problem. These must be ruled out before proceeding with any behavior modification program. Have your aggressive behaving dog thoroughly vetted, especially if the onset of the aggression was sudden. Rage Syndrome and other epilepsies, severe pancreatitis, or the side effects of drugs used to treat various illnesses such as skin allergies, all can cause aggressive behavior. In the drug department, steroids are most often the culprits. A second, common pharmaceutical cause of aggression is seizure or other medications that make your dog drowsy or disoriented. If you or your veterinarian suspect a health problem is the cause of your dog's aggressive behavior, consult with a veterinarian that specializes in behavior modification. (If you are unable to find one in your area, contact the University of Pennsylvania Veterinary School.)

OK, your canine hoodlum was abused as a puppy, and he only growls in certain situations. He has good reason to be aggressive toward children because he was tormented by them while chained in the backyard of his former home. Bully hates men because his first, second, third owner's boyfriend smacked him around when he had accidents on the floor and so forth. These things are a shame to have happened and valid reasons for the behaviors, but they do not make aggression acceptable. Just like people that suffered rotten childhoods, we can understand the reasons behind their antisocial behaviors, but that does not excuse them from learning to act better. In fact, your canine hoodlum must reform, for he or she is much more likely to suffer the death penalty than his or her human counterpart. Do you think that an extreme or melodramatic statement? I can tell you from years of experience and training thousands of dogs that aggressive behaviors snowball. Seldom does Bully live out a full lifetime only growling over his food. If he gets away with it, next Bully will extend his kitchen space not to just his bowl but to the to foot area surrounding it. Then it will be do not get on *his* couch when he is sleeping on it and so on until you have a monster on your hands. There is a point of no return, a line, once crossed, when it is no longer possible to reform the aggressive dog. Then what? Give him to someone else? Who will want him. Its death row!

Even if you do find someone to take your hoodlum, you may still be legally liable if he bites in his new home! He is most likely going to wind up at the pound alone, scared, and put to death in a terrifying environment. And you know what? It is not his fault! There are very, very few truly psychotic dogs. Those should be humanly euthanized by the owners' veterinarian, ideally with the owners present to comfort the dog. Nearly all aggressive dogs are created by humans through genetics and environment. You have an obligation to select a breed or mix you can handle, and train your pet in such a way that he can live in today's society.

Since the root of aggressive behavior in most animals (two legged and four) is insecurity and fear, the solution to the problem is building self confidence and self control. You guessed it…good solid obedience training. Whether your dog is running in fear or charging, the answer is the same. If Bully will hold a sit-stay in the face of whatever scares him, he will have the opportunity to learn that his monsters are not harmful at all (of course, it is your responsibility to make sure this is true). Moreover, if Bully will hold a sit-stay instead of charging, he is using self control to break his antisocial habit pattern.

Obedience training is the key to resolving aggression problems, whether the problem is the result of a genetic flaw or environmental. If the problem is largely due to poor breeding, the likelihood of success is diminished in comparison to a dog in which the aggression is a learned behavior or due to a lack of socialization. The age of the onset of the aggressive behavior is the best indicator of its source. If your dog has exhibited even minor aggressive tendencies from a very young age, the indication would be it is an inherited personality trait. If your dog was perfectly friendly and completely non-threatening until later in life, most likely his bad attitude is learned.

OK, your dog has an aggression problem. But, whether you created the monster or you inherited it from someone else, it now falls

upon you to reform him. First and foremost, is strict obedience training. It is the clearest way to establish your dominance. Next you must
make your dog defer to rights as a leader in many subtle ways outlined in the Pack Psychology chapter, such as no human food, no
sleeping on your bed, through all doorways behind his human pack
leader, submitting to and establishing good eye contact, moving out
of your way, and responding immediately to a couple of surprise
downs a day. An aggressive dog should be trailing a leash or 6 feet of
rope (if you think he might chew up his expensive leash) at all times.
This will allow you to get hold of your dog safely.

Many dogs growl when you reach for their collars. The collar
represents control, something they may not wish to relinquish. This
is easily handled by having your dog trail a six foot leash or six feet
of rope (cotton clothesline works well). An aggressive dog should
have the leash or rope on when whenever a human is present. As a
safety precaution, remove the lead when your dog is going to be
home alone. If necessary, piece of rope is easily soaked in Grannick's
Bitter Apple to discourage chewing. The trailing line allows you to
safely and quickly get a hold of your dog when necessary for correction.

To correct a minor aggressive behavior, prepare a squirt gun or
spray bottle that shoots a stream containing 1/4 white vinegar and 3/4
water. Do not recycle a bottle that has contained a commercial
cleaner. Any residue may injure your dogs eyes should you miss your
target, his mouth. You may increase this mixture to 1/2/ and 1/2 but
it is usually not necessary. Use only white vinegar. Cider vinegar contains sediment that might irritate your dog's eyes. The vinegar and
water is used to correct aggression by squirting your hoodlum in the
mouth several times. His mouth is what growls and bites. Dogs do
not like the taste of vinegar. They quickly figure out that if they keep
their mouth shut that nasty tasting stuff can't get in there. This makes
a very direct connection to deter the aggression. If you miss and get
the solution in your dog's eyes, it may sting but it will not injure his
eyes.

At any sign of aggression, step on or grab the trailing rope or
leash, squirt your dog several times in the mouth with the vinegar
solution. Then immediately put him on a down-stay. When you "put
your dog down," you are doing just that, asserting your dominance

and sending the message, "I am the pack leader and I will not tolerate that behavior!" Caution! Be careful when correcting an aggressive dog!

On to specific situations. There are several forms of possessive aggression, the most common of which is aggression over food. If your dog growls (or snaps) over his food, for one week add something tasty to your dog's bowl after he has started eating his regular meal. Just casually walk by and drop the tasty morsel in. No lecture. No, "look what mommy has for you!'" Just drop the treat in Brat's bowl and continue on your way. (Do not get your hands down close to the dog's bowl.) This will teach your dog that you are not going to steal his food. Therefore, there is no need to guard it. The next week, pick up Brat's tailing leash before giving him his bowl of food (feed meals, do not leave food out all the time). After Brat has started eating, command him to sit and stay. Take his bowl up. If you are afraid he might bite before you can stop him with the leash, use a stick or broom handle to slide his bowl away until you are more confident. This will keep your face as well as your hands out of harm's way. Correct your dog if he breaks the stay. Use the vinegar solution as outlined above if there is even the slightest display of aggression (silently raising his lip over just one tooth qualifies). Do not forget to follow up with a down-stay! If there is no display of aggression or after Brat has held the down-stay for one to three minutes, release him from the stay and give him back his food. If there was no aggression, let your dog finish his meal in peace. If there was any display of aggression, remove his bowl again after putting him on a sit-stay. Repeat until you succeed.

The next several meals, just add something tasty to your dog's bowl as you did the first week. After several days have passed, go through the procedure of removing your dog's bowl again. Work in this pattern until you can remove your dog's food while he is eating with no sign of aggression for at least two sessions. *Do not forget to just add some tasty morsel for several days between attempts to remove your dog's bowl. Mealtime should not become a stressful event on a daily basis!* Then give it a rest for a week or so and try again. If there is no aggression after a week off, consider the issue resolved but test Brat once in a while to make sure he does not backslide.

Resolving the problem of growling over a sleeping place is similar. First of all you must strictly establish that furniture is for humans and floors are for canine hoodlums. (See the chapter on getting on the furniture). If your dog acts aggressively when you walk by him on the floor, step on his trailing leash, squirt him in the mouth with the vinegar solution and put Brat on a down-stay in another spot (out of the flow of traffic…remember you should not walk around your dog, see pack psychology chapter). Moving your dog from his chosen spot dethrones him.

Aggression over stolen or otherwise forbidden objects (such as bones) as well as your dog's own toys is similarly handled. Get hold of the trailing leash and put your dog on a sit-stay. Command your dog to drop the object. If he does not, place your hand across the top of his muzzle and squeeze his lips in between the teeth of his upper and lower jaws. Your dog will not bite through his own lips unless he is truly crazy. Remove the object from your dog's mouth with your free hand. Correct any aggression with several squirts of the vinegar solution. Correct the broken stay if necessary.

Grooming is another situation in which aggression often occurs. To teach your dog to be polite for brushing, Place him on a sit or down-stay *on leash.* Brush gently for just one to two minutes. Release your dog from the stay and reward him with a treat and lots of praise. This is one situation where I consistently use a food reward for good behavior. The next day, brush for just one minute longer. Gradually build up to the amount of time necessary to thoroughly groom your dog. If your dog breaks the stay, use the appropriate correction. If your dog shows even the slightest sign of aggression, squirt him in the mouth several times with the vinegar solution and follow up with a brief down-stay. Release your dog from the down-stay, place him/her on another stay (sit or down) and resume brushing.

Make sure you are not causing your dog any unnecessary discomfort. Do not use a metal toothed comb or brush on the bony parts of your dog's face or legs. Do not pull her hair any more than absolutely necessary. Brush your dog regularly so he does not have mats that are uncomfortable to have removed. Proper grooming tools will make the task easier on both you and your dog. (See the chapter on grooming).

Nail clipping is a particularly aggravating procedure to many dogs. I believe some dogs start off not liking to have their feet handled because they are ticklish. Then somebody (we all do it occasionally) "quicks" the dog a couple of times (cuts the nail too short into the blood vessel and nerve). And Vois La`! You have a dog that is aggressive when you try to cut his nails. Another possible ingredient in making dogs aggressive over nail clipping is inadvertently cranking Buster's leg into an uncomfortable position. Particularly in dogs with joint problems, such inadvertence may trigger an aggressive response.

The preventive medicine, TTouch, (See the chapter on TTouch) is also part of the remodeling plan. The first step to desensitize your dog to having his feet handled is to start TTouch away from the feet and gradually working your way down to being able to "touch" your dog's feet without contention. Next, using TTouch, introduce the nail clipper by brushing it over the foot. Do not try to clip a nail until your dog accepts the clipper without contention. When your dog accepts the clipper and is completely relaxed when you handle his feet, you are ready to clip his first nail.

Place Brat on a sit-stay, clip the very tip of one nail. The point is not to properly trim the nail but to be able to clip it without aggression from your dog. If there is no aggression, release your dog from the stay and make a big fuss over him including giving him his favorite dog cookie. This is one of the few situations I regularly use a food reward. If there is any aggression, use the vinegar solution followed by a down-stay. Then try again. One way or another, clip one nail. You must not quit until you win. Wait 24 hours before clipping one more nail.

You can use a similar procedure to teach your dog to be compliant with ear cleaning and tooth scaling.

For some owners, perhaps the most distressing form of dog aggression is that toward non-family members, company in your home or people you meet on the street. As discussed earlier this problem is often a result of shyness, lack of socialization, lack of proper training, genetics, abuse, or a combination of these causes. There is sometimes another factor in the development of aggression toward non-family members. It is the attitude of the dog's owner. Some people get a warped ego thrill from their dog acting aggressive and

encourage the behavior for this reason. A timid owner may unconsciously encourage aggression out of their own fear of the world.
Most often aggression is improperly encouraged because dog owners
want protection for their home and family and of course, there is
nothing wrong in that. However, if a dog is well bred and of sound
mind, this encouragement is not necessary. It is a dog's nature to protect pack and territory. If an owner overly encourages protectiveness
in their dog, an uncontrolled aggression problem may develop. You
may need the help of a qualified professional trainer to determine if
your attitude and behavior has contributed to your dog's bad acting
and to educate yourself on how best to improve. If your dog's aggression toward non-family members is even slightly more than very
minor, get qualified professional help! This is a lawsuit waiting to
happen. In the eyes of the law, obedience training is viewed favorable
because you are building and exerting control of your dog. On the
other hand, any form of aggression (or guard) training <u>decreases</u> a
dog's inhibition to bite and therefore, makes the owner <u>more</u> culpa-
ble.

    If your dog is in the very early stage of showing aggression
toward non-family members, you MUST train your dog on the five
basic commands (heel, sit, stay, down come) until he will perform
them consistently in distracting situations on one command only.
Your dog should have enough self control to hold a 30 minute down-
stay around distractions (such as in your veterinarians waiting room)
without repeated commands. If these goals elude you, work on them!
If your dog has been properly trained but allowed to backslide, brush
up his basic obedience training. A dog that has an aggression problem is most likely not a good candidate for a group obedience class.
Get private lessons or send Brat off to boarding school.

    Once your dominance and control has been established through
proper training, you can tackle the aggression problem if it still
exists. Often minor problems of many behaviors diminish or are
completely resolved through the training without the need to directly
correct the behavior. If the aggression problem is still in evidence
after training, you will have the foundation and tools to correct the
problem. If your dog is growling or lunging at people on the street,
use right about-turns to get her attention off the passerby and refo-
cused on you. Then put your dog on a stay to build her self control

around the trigger for the aggression (in this situation, the Passerby). Set up a situation for brat in which you find someone willing and able to follow directions and become a Passerby...someone who won't sue you. Armed with a vinegar squirt bottle and a treat, put your dog on a sit-stay and have Passerby approach your dog. If your dog breaks the stay, correct. If your dog shows even the slightest aggression, squirt her in the mouth several times with the vinegar solution, and put your dog on a short down-stay. Break your dog out of the down-stay and put her on a sit-stay. Have Passerby approach again. Repeat this procedure until your dog allows the approach without aggression or breaking the stay. Reward with lavish praise and <u>one</u> treat. And quit until the next day. Then try it again.

Next step is to be able to have Passerby pet your dog very briefly. Follow the same procedure of approach and add having Passerby present his or her hand palm open, fingers pointing down for the dog to sniff. Palm open, the hand is wider therefore harder for your dog to get a good bite, and fingers pointing down is non-threatening. If that goes well, Passerby may briefly (one stroke) pet your dog on top of the head or under the chin, whichever your dog prefers. If that goes well, have Passerby (not you) give your dog a small treat. You praise the dog as if she just gave you a million dollars. Quit until the next day. Then try it again. Continue with baby steps, increasing the length of petting and then progressing to strangers on the street. At any point there is aggression from your dog, correct as outlined and drop back a step. As soon as that step has been successfully completed, bump it up a notch. <u>BE CAREFUL!</u>

Let's look at handling aggression toward visitors in your home. Read the chapter on jumping specifically on how to do introductions. Have <u>ALL</u> company (yes, even Mom and your steady) knock, and wait for you to answer the door when they come to visit. Deadlock the door if necessary to enforce this rule. Before you open the door, put Brat on leash on a a sit-stay far enough back from the door for you to open it fully, room for the visitor to enter and for you to correct your dog. Follow a scenario similar to the one outlined for greetings on the street. Set up a situation for Brat similar to your agreement with the Passerby, this time we will call him Vistor. Armed with a vinegar squirt bottle and some treats, put your dog on a sit-stay and have your Visitor enter your house. If your dog breaks the stay, correct. If your dog shows even the slightest aggression, squirt her in the mouth several times with the vinegar solution and put your dog on a short down-stay. Have Visitor back outside and shut the door. Break your dog out of the down-stay and put her on a sit-stay. Have Visitor knock again and enter at your invitation. Repeat this procedure until your dog allows Visitor to enter without breaking the stay. Reward with lavish praise. Next have Visitor present his or her hand palm open fingers pointing down for the dog to sniff. If that goes well, Visitor may briefly (one stroke) pet your dog on top of the head or under the chin which ever your dog prefers. If that goes well, have Visitor (not you) give your dog a small treat. You praise your dog lavishly. Heel your dog into the living room (or wherever) and put her on a down-stay close enough to you that you can easily correct her but not so close that she will feel protective of you. Do not place the dog in the path of traffic. If your dog breaks the down-stay or shows aggression, correct appropriately. At the end of your company's visit, heel your dog to the door and place her on a sit-stay to allow Visitor to depart unmolested. If your dog behaved well, make sure to let her know!!! <u>BE CAREFUL!</u>

After several successful visits, try releasing your dog from the down-stay in the living room after about ten minutes. Leave the leash on your dog! If she is non-threatening, let your dog be on his own until it is time for your company to depart. Then heel your dog to the door and put her on a sit-stay as before. If at any point after being released from her down-stay, your dog becomes threatening, grab the leash and correct with the vinegar solution. Put her on another down-stay until it is time for your company to depart. Your dog lost her right to be on her own time(off the down-stay) by her bad behavior. Dogs are highly intelligent and do make these kind of associations!

These are the most common situations in which pets become aggressive. The procedures outlined here can be adapted to other situations. Sometimes a stronger correction may be necessary. They should only be attempted by or under the guidance of a qualified professional dog trainer. Under correcting frequently makes the aggressive dog worst because she is winning. Don't start what you are not willing to carry through. Get help!

BARKING AND WHINING

Dogs bark for a wide variety of reasons—some good, some bad. Dogs have different sounding barks for different situations. Barking is often born of fear as seen in shy dogs. When I moved to Delaware, I learned to discern a special bark of fear, "There is a snake in my kennel!" (Quite harmless black snakes, I can assure *you*, but the dogs didn't think so !) It is generally not considered a problem for a dog to give a few yaps of joy in greeting his or her owner or in play. Most owners appreciate their dog's alarm bark warning them of intruders. Barking to ask to go outside to relieve themselves is also acceptable. However, any of these barks can become excessive and annoying. Barking to beg for food or attention is a problem. From a trainer's viewpoint, protest barking ("barking back") is a serious warning of a budding aggression problem. The next step is often growling which is the precursor to a snap and so forth.

Finally, all too often, barking is a desperate attempt of the chained dog to relieve the frustration, loneliness, and boredom of the cruel isolation from his pack. Yes, I said cruel! Dogs are highly social animals. Under normal conditions of the wild pack, a dog has a lot of company twenty-four hours a day. In a domestic situation, the humans and other animals in the household form a dog's pack. To be chained by the neck in the back yard is worse than solitary confinement because the dog has the frustration of watching the world go by. Your dog may have more square feet of space on a chain, but it is much less frustrating to be confined to a pen (10 X 20 feet is a good size for the medium to large dog…Lab). In a pen, the dog has a visual barrier of the fence, on a chain he has the illusion of freedom. It makes a difference psychologically, therefore, behaviorally to the dog. *Whenever you are home, the dog should be with you.* Think of it in terms of your being in prison. I don't care how nice the cell is if you are isolated from those you love for 23 of 24 hours, it is a miserable life.

OK, you are doing it all right. The dog is in a nice outside kennel or is in the house when you are gone, in when you are home, and has been through basic obedience training, but you have a barking problem. The first step in resolution is to determine why your dog is barking.

Let's first look at situations where barks of joy have gotten out of hand. If your dog gets carried away in greeting, the answer is obedience training. Remember this phrase, "Whenever he is giving you the least in self-control, you demand the most, a stay." When you come through the door, get a collar (if your dog is not wearing one) and a tab or leash, as necessary, on your dog and insist on a sit-stay. If your dog barks on a stay, squirt him in the mouth with a mixture of 1/4 white vinegar and 3/4 water. Use a clean (new) spray bottle that shoots a strong stream or a good squirt gun. Never us a bottle that contained a cleaner as the residue may injure the eyes. Of course, you are aiming for the mouth (that is what barks), but if you miss and get the eyes, this formula will not injure your dog's eyes. I have used a solution as strong as 1/2 white vinegar (do not use cider vinegar as it contains sediment which may irritate the eyes) and 1/2 water without eye irritation. However, if your dog's eyes appear irritated, discontinue. If your dog breaks the stay when he is squired, correct the broken stay. He set up the situation, he must endure the consequences.

Use the same procedure if your dog gets overly excited when company departs. Put him on a leash and a sit-stay. Use the squirt bottle as necessary but do not use it as a cure-all for everything. The vinegar solution squirt bottle is only for offenses committed by the mouth…barking, growling, aggression. If overused, you dog will become immune to it. Barking during departures can evolve into nips in the butt of the exiting party. So do not let this behavior get out of hand.

If your pup gets too loud during play, stop the game. Put him on a short sit or down-stay. Try playing some more. Do this 3–4 times.

If he cannot maintain some level of self-control, stop playing for the time being. After a few sessions of stopping play 3–4 times by having the dog hold a stay when the barking becomes excessive and/or stopping play altogether, it will dawn on Buster to control his loud mouth in play.

Although, protectiveness in a dog is desirable, it can go overboard. At a seminar I attended, a woman proclaimed that her rare-breed guard dog alarm-barked when someone moved _in the neighbors house!_ Not a dog I would want to live with. When your dog alarm barks at the approach of someone to *your house*, thank him. Praise after a few barks and then command him "That's enough!" (or a similar phrase). The word "enough" when said roughly sounds like a growl, so you may get an instinctive response of quieting. Then insist on his being quiet by putting him on a stay. If your dog barks on a stay, squirt him in the mouth with vinegar water.

Barking or whining for attention or when begging for food should be ended by a down-stay. The down is a submissive posture in dog psychology. When you "put your dog down" you are telling him that you are the pack leader and will not tolerate inappropriate behavior. Use the vinegar and water squirt if the nuisance barks or whines on the stay. Correct the stay if your dog breaks it when squirted.

A special note about whining. Do let this very aggravating habit take hold. It can become unconscious on the part of your dog. What your dog is NOT consciously aware he is doing cannot be corrected. Once whining has progressed to the point of being an unconscious habit, the dog must first be made aware of the behavior before reforming it can begin. You will need qualified professional help. Sometimes this habit is not possible to resolve in older dogs.

Remember, in correcting excessively barking or any other behavior problem, the base line of behavior generally increases before it decreases, once you start correction. The behavior has worked in the past. So an animal's (two legged and four) first response is usually to try more of the same behavior. Be consistent. It will work if you persist. Dogs are quick learners if consequences are consistent. In a well-trained dog, you will most likely see improvement in a minor to moderate barking problem within a week, resolution to the problem in about two weeks. Keep in mind that a critical learning period in dogs (how long it takes to habituate a new behavior or diminish an old one) is approximately two weeks. Just like humans, some dogs learn a little faster or more slowly than others. However, even for the canine geniuses, a behavior modification program should be carried out for at least two weeks just to make sure. Slacking off too soon will mean having to start all over again and it is usually more difficult the second time around because the dog won the first round!

BEGGING

Although hand feeding will teach dogs to beg, some develop this rude habit that have never had human food either by hand or from their dog pan. Remember your canine pal has an acute sense of smell. Even if Rover never tasted a pork chop, he can tell by the smell it would be delicious.

When raising a puppy or during the period of establishment of house rules with a secondhand dog, do not give him <u>any</u> human food. Feeding human food confuses the pack order. In the wild, the pack leaders make the kill and eat the best parts before other pack members eat. The underlings eat the leftovers! Your dog is not a member of a wolf pack, but of a mixed pack consisting of the humans and other pets, if any in your home. The translation of the rule of the wild pack that the pack leader eats the best parts first is, in the mixed pack, humans eat human food and dogs eat dog food.

Later when your pup is a well-behaved adult or your second-hand dog is a very well-behaved family member, you can give some table scraps (talk to your vet if your dog has any health problems). Give both veggie and meat scraps to maintain balance in your dogs diet. Remember too much fat can make your dog ill, sometimes seriously. Feed table scraps in your dog's pan so he understands that what he is allowed to eat always comes from his bowl only. Do not let Rover clean the dinner plates and then be surprised when you find him licking plates while they are still on the table!

All right, what do you do if in spite of your good, or not so good, efforts to prevent begging, Rover is a beggar. You can send him down to the street corner with a tin cup (my brother used to give his dog,

Rover, a bag to carry trick or treating…Tom got twice as much candy!), or you can take control. Stop the feeding of anything but dog food and that <u>from his pan only</u>. No hand-fed dog treats until Rover is reformed. And humans must eat at the table for the time being at least. Put your dog on a down-stay during meals. He can't beg if he is on a leash length (a polite but accessible distance for correction) down stay from the dinner table. After you have established a good spot for Rover during meals, using the same place every time, you may advance from a down-stay to "go lay down."

(Go lay down means go to your place and stay there until further notice. It should be a part of basic obedience, taught and trained thoroughly).

BOUNDARY TRAINING

Ah! The myth of the peaceful dog laying contentedly hour after hour on the front porch faithfully protecting his master's home until he or she returns home from a hard day's work.

Let's get a grip. A dog is a predator designed to roam his territory in search of game. Where do you thing the name "Rover" game from? Yes, I can leave my dog outside in an unfenced area and most of the time he'll be laying on the back porch when I go to call him in. And yes, he knows not to go past a certain point in the driveway without me and my permission (he automatically waits at the invisible line while I get the mail from the mailbox). Would my dog ever venture off that porch or heaven forbid, cross that line, you bet ya! if the motivation was strong enough. When he first goes out, my dog has to attend to the business of checking out the neighborhood. Is the groundhog in that hole by the back pasture? What about hunting a few pesky rats by the hay bales and the Beagles next door? Wonder if those Beagles can tell any tales of recent hunts. OK, all is well and I need a nap. Guess I'll head for the back porch! And that boundary line before the road? Yes, he knows the rule and better than most, but that hunter looks threatening. What is he doing at the edge of the front yard? Better chase him off before he does harm. Get the picture?

Even the most sound boundary training has limited use. So should we forget about boundary training? No, absolutely not, but you must realistically recognize limitations, especially if you live in suburbia. The closer your home to the road, the less safe it is to depend on boundary training.

Some breeds are more or less homebodies than others. Hunting/sporting breeds are generally more likely to roam. Rotties, German Shepherd Dogs, and certain other guard breeds are more likely to stay home and guard their territory. However, not only is it illegal in most areas to leave dogs loose outdoors, do you really want to risk the possibility of a lawsuit if Butch breaks the boundary line and accosts someone? Some things are training issues, some are not.

Molly, my first "dog of a lifetime" was extremely well boundary trained. In seven years, she only broke her boundary training twice. Once to ward off a stray dog that was threatening to attack a child in her yard and once following one of "her" kids (my partner's son) to visit a neighbor. Both incidences involved her crossing a dangerous road. She could have easily been killed either time. The point is only <u>two</u> mistakes in seven years (I moved after that) is an extremely good record, but still could have resulted in her death.

OK, you understand the limitations of boundary training, but still believe as I do, that it may be of some value in your situation. How do you do it? First your dog must be reliably off-leashed trained. Ultimately boundary training is off-leash control, even though it is initially taught and trained on leash and light line. If your dog is not solidly off-leash trained, she certainly cannot be boundary trained!!!!

Next, decide on where the boundaries should be. Do not make the edge of a road a boundary. Make it twenty feet back from the road. If there is not a natural visual barrier (hedge, flower line), put up one. Kite string and plant stakes are sufficient. The visual barrier is more for you than your dog. Dogs are very accurate (much-more-so than most humans) at measuring distance. If one day you train to an imaginary line that is twenty feet from the road and the next day you train it fifteen feet from the road, you will confuse your dog and impede the training.

Now that you have visual barriers at all of boundaries you wish to teach and train your dog to respect, take your very obedient off-leash trained dog out on a six foot training lead. Heel around the inside of the boundaries in both directions. Do this for about a week or until you think Rover has the idea. Then start practicing stays where you cross the boundary, but of course, your dog does not.

For boundary training to be most effective, your dog should never be allowed to cross the boundaries accept in a car. However, this may not be practical in your situation as it was not in mine. Mitch and I walked regularly in the State Park across the street from our property over the boundary line to which he has been trained. If you have a similar situation where you need to create a spot from which your dog may exit his boundaries with you, with your permission, it is best to have only <u>one</u> exit. The more exits, the weaker the boundary training (remember ideally there would be no exits). Teach your dog that he may cross his boundary at this spot only by leaving your dog on a stay and crossing the boundary. Call your dog. Make it a formal recall as taught in obedience school. You are giving your dog permission to break the stay and the boundary by your command to come.

Train your dog that she may only cross that boundary when you call her by setting up situations to proof the training. Have someone else (not a family member) try calling your dog across the boundary while you have her on a stay. Have someone jog, ride a bike, horse, walk a dog past your dog while she is on a stay inside her boundaries both at the point of exit (if you have one) and in other places. Of course you will firmly correct if your dog breaks the stay. Also, have family members walk off your property across the boundaries while your dog is on a stay. Remember, a family member should not give conflicting commands by calling your dog, but he or she may certainly walk by.

After completing a couple of weeks of training at this level, or whenever your dog seems to comprehend the boundaries and is not breaking stays, graduate to a thirty-foot leash. Leave your dog on a stay facing a boundary and go out behind him to the end of the lead. Have a really tempting pre-planned distraction to appear suddenly. Firmly correct if your dog breaks the stay. Work around all the boundaries this way with new distractions. Now try setting your dog up with distractions when he is not on a stay.

The final step is using a light line in place of the thirty-foot lead. A light line is 1/8 of an inch in diameter nylon line with died to match the training environment. Tie several sets of knots in one end to prevent the line's slipping from underfoot when you step on it to prevent your dog's escape. Let your dog trail the light line for several days until he is ignoring it. Then arrange for new, even more tempting distractions. Once you are confident in your dog's boundary training, you may remove the light line.Please remember not to unnecessarily risk your dog's life by inappropriately depending on your boundary training. Did you do the best of boundary training possible?

BREED COUNSELING...COULD IT BE A MISMATCH?

Too often dogs came into my training center because they were mismatched with their owners. Primarily this happens because people pick their pets based on appearance. That is like picking your spouse based on appearance. "Pretty is as pretty does." If you live in an apartment, a Beagle bred to have a voice is not a good choice. If you have a lot of people casually wander in and out of your house, a guardbreed is not a good choice. The most common mismatch is a high energy sporting breed in the average suburban home. High energy dogs require extensive exercise, and that does not, mean just being out in the backyard.

Many differences between an owner's personality and lifestyle and the genetic disposition of a dog may be resolved with training, or at least the two of you may reach a viable compromise. If your mismatch is too great, you and your dog may be better off parting ways. However, this should be a very last resort! Your dog did not ask to belong to you, and it is your responsibility to to try everything possible before considering placing your dog in another home. It is also your responsibility to find your dog a suitable home. DO NOT dump your dog at the local shelter!!!

The following questionnaire may initiate a thoughtful choice of a suitable breed for you. If you already have a dog, it may give you some insight into existing problems. Complete the questionnaire and research breeds, the one you have or those you are considering getting. Remember to investigate various breeds with all breed professionals such as your veterinarian, dog groomer, boarding kennel operator, etc. If you only research a breed through its breeders, you will get a very one-sided viewpoint.

BREED COUNSELING

Human Needs

1. Who is the dog for?
2. Would you consider yourself (each family member) demonstrative or reserved in your physical and emotional attitudes towards a dog?
3. Are children (your future ones, grandchildren, neighborhood children) going to be around the dog on a regular basis?
4. Do you like to play games with dogs?
5. Do you want to teach your dog tricks?
6. Do you like a puppyish or a dignified attitude in dogs?
7. Would you like your dog to be constantly around you?
8. Is anyone in your family allergic to dogs or other animals?
9. Would you consider yourself to be a perfectionist?
10. Do <u>other people</u> consider you to be a patient person? Do you consider yourself to be patient?
11. Do you enjoy being around people or animals who <u>physically</u> respond quickly and precisely?
12. Are there any breeds or types of dogs you are afraid of?
13. Are there any family members who are:

____highly nervous ____extremely shy____hyperactive
____heavy handed ____elderly and frail ____mentally handicapped
____physically handicapped

14. Is there anyone in the family who is opposed to getting a dog?

The Nature of the Dog

1. Barking:
    A. Do you dislike:

        ____High pitched
        ____Low pitched
        ____Howls
        ____Whines

    B. Amount of Noise:

        ____As little as possible
        ____Moderate
        ____Lots of barking

2. Protection Dogs:
Protection dogs break into 3 GENERAL groups:
    1) The Alarm Dog (only barks, rarely bites, likes people)
    2) The Threat Dog (although it appears threatening, it usually is all bluff)
    3) The Attack Dog, natural or trained (will bite, very protective, weapon)

Are any of the above desirable to you?_____ which?_____

Is protection the basic reason you want a dog?_____

If yes, would you replace a dog who failed as protection?_____

If no, would you replace a dog who was protective?_____

Do non-family members including small children come and go freely into your yard or home?_____ Do they let themselves in?_____

3. Special Needs:

Do you plan to hunt with your dog?_____
    What game?_____

Do you need the dog for handicapped
    assistance?_____

Do you plan to show in obedience?_____ In
    Breed?_____

Will the dog be a traveling
    companion?_____

Other:_____
    Will you replace the dog if it cannot fulfill these special needs?
    _____

The Dog's Appearance

1. Size Preferred:

    ____Tiny—under 12 lbs. (Chihuahua)
    ____Small—12–25 lbs. (Cocker)
    ____Medium—25–50 lbs. (Springer Spaniel)
    ____Large—50–100 lbs. (German Shepherd)
    ____Giant—(St. Bernard)

If you have a specific size in mind, indicate that. If you have a
    range of acceptable sizes, indicate the range.

2. Coat Type:____Smooth (Doberman)

    ____Wire Haired (Wire Haired Fox Terrier)
    ____Medium/plush coat—(German Shepherd)
    ____Feathered (Irish Setter)
    ____Long (Collie)
    ____Shaggy (Lhasa)
    ____"Hairless" (Chinese Crested)
    ____"Non Shedding" (Poodle)

A "non-shedding" coat is hair which grows like human hair. There
is some shedding and this coat type requires cutting and grooming. Please indicate all acceptable coat type(s).

3. Do you have a preference for a male or female dog?
    _____

4. Do you plan to spay or castrate your dog? _____ If no, would
    that answer change if neutering would prevent or stop behav-
    ioral or physical problems?_____

5. If the perfect dog for your situation would be an adult instead of
    a puppy, would you consider getting an
    adult?_____

6. What is the most striking dog you have ever seen?
    _____

7. Do you have <u>strong</u> preferences regarding the following physi-
    cal traits:

Please rate "L" (like), "D" (dislike), or "N" (neutral)

   A. Ears:Erect_____ Hound_____
   B. Mouth:Dry_____ Wet_____
   D. Tail:Short_____Long_____ Curled_____
   E. Coat Colors:Like_____
       Dislike_____F. Eye color:
       Dark_____Light_____ Blue_
   G. Face: Long Muzzle_____
       Short Muzzle_____
   H. Body typeStocky_____
       Elegant_____
   I. Snoring or snorting _____

The Dog's Environment

1. Do you have a securely fenced
    yard?_____

2. Will the dog be primarily an indoor pet, an out door pet or
    both?_____

3. When indoors, will the dog be allowed free access to all parts of the house when it is trained?

   _____

4. Are your floors primarily car-peted?_____

5. Do you currently have ANY other pets? _____
   Describe:_____

   _____

6. Is someone usually at home? If not, how many hours a day will the dog spend alone?_____

7. If you do not have a fenced yard, how regularly will the dog get a high amount of exercise outdoors? (be honest)

   _____

   NOTES:

CAR SICKNESS

Car sickness is most common in puppies. Pups have good reason for getting upset during automobile rides. A puppy's first car ride is generally when she is stolen away from her mother and litter mates. The next several rides are to the veterinarian's to get stabbed with sharp pointy objects that make her feel ill. Who would not feel like puking at the next outing?

Prevention and cure are the same for car sickness. Take your puppy or older dog that suffers from car sickness for some short positive rides. Stop the car **before** your dog gets sick. Take him out of the car for on a little walk or play ball for a few minutes before getting back in the car and returning home. Stopping and getting out helps your dog get his land legs under him and calm down. The walk or game of fetch teach him that a car ride does not always end in a negative experience.

You may have to start out by driving only one block before stopping. Gradually increase the distance you drive before stopping, but only as your dog can handle the increased distance with out getting sick. If your dog gets sick during the process, you may have to start all over at the shortest distance. So do not rush.

Some dogs benefit from the use of a motion sickness drug in conjunction with the program outlined above. If your dog salivates excessively before vomiting, often stopping the salivation with a drug called atropine will help the dog get over the problem more effectively than Dramamine. However, some veterinarians are reluctant to prescribe atropine. You will have to consult with yours.

CAT CHASING

Oh boy! Dogs just naturally like to chase kitties. It can range from harmless play to a deadly hunt. Often cat chasing starts out as a game and progresses into a fatal predatory behavior. Fatal for the cat and sometimes the dog, put to death for this problem or hit by a car during the chase. Its best to stop the play before it becomes a hunt.

I have put a stop to this behavior with varying degrees of correction from a few scoldings, to a series of properly executed right about turns, to the use of very strong (but humane) deterrents. I once reformed a dog who had killed nine cats! After school, his owner sent me a photo of him napping with his new kitty. On the other end of the spectrum, I personally owned a brilliant competition dog who could not be reformed. I ran the gambit of corrections to no avail. After he killed my second cat, I placed him in a cat free home where he was much loved, and lived happily ever after. He even went on to be a children's therapy dog.

Some breeds have a propensity for cat killing, German Short-haired Pointers, German Shepherds, and Siberian Huskies (although they prefer rabbits if given the choice). If you own a pup of one of these breeds or a mixture of them, be on your toes to prevent the problem. Puppies can be taught to be gentle with other small fury creatures by socializing them together and discouraging any rough play. If you have an older dog that is a cat chaser, especially of the above mentioned genetic heritage, reforming the behavior may require professional help or it may not be possible even with professional help. Prevention is, as always, the best medicine.

If you are working with a young pup that has started chasing the cat, hope that the cat turns around and smacks your pup a few good ones. This is very effective. Short of Garfield's correcting the little bundle of joy, try a gentle scruff shake and a mild scolding every time your pup takes off after kitty. Having your pup trail a short piece of clothes line (cheaply replaced when chewed) makes it easy to stop the chase. A scruff shake is performed by grasping your pup by the scruff (loose skin on the back of the neck), elevating his front feet off the floor a couple of inches, and gently but firmly shaking him from side to side once or twice. Not too violently!!! If your scare the wits out of your pup, he will have none to make the connection between his chasing kitty and the negative consequence. Scruff shakes should only be used in young puppies and sparingly so. If overused you may either teach your pup to be frightened of you or teach him to ignore you, depending on the severity of the shakes.

Scruff shakes are ineffective in older pups (4 months being roughly the division depending on the individual's temperament). Ineffective correction often makes a problem worse. The pup, a highly intelligent animal (some scientists compare a dog's intelligence level with that of a 3–6 year old child!), will realize that you are trying to take control and are not able to do so. He is winning! This is worse than no correction.

I teach my own young pups the meaning of "no" with a scruff shake. When "no" is properly taught, it means simply to stop whatever you are presently doing. It should then be followed by instruction on something positive to do. If "no" is properly taught its effectiveness is not dependent on a loud or harsh tone of voice. All commands should be spoken in a normal tone and volume. Shouting or speaking in a threatening voice creates stress in the speaker as well as the receiver. If you do not believe this, pay attention to your stomach muscles the next time you yell at the dog or the kids. We all have enough stress in our lives without creating any unnecessarily. The only time I yell at dogs is to be heard over their barking or growling, or if the environment is very noisy.

OK, back to Flash the cat chaser. If you have an older pup or adult dog, set him up around cats and work a series of right about turns (taught in basic obedience training if you got quality instruction) until he no longer takes his eyes off you to look at kitty. You may have to start a fair distance away from the cat if Flash is very intent on cat killing. Work the turns repeatedly as you move closer and closer to your distraction, the cat. Do not move in closer until Flash is focused on you at each 2–3 foot increment. As soon as your dog's attention is off you and on the cat, whether at 40 feet or 3 feet, make an appropriately sharp right about turn. Try again at that distance. If your dog's attention remains on you, go a little closer and so forth. Work like this in different locations with different cats. Put the cat in a cage if necessary to get him to cooperate and for his protection if you are unsure of your agility in correcting your dog. If you need help, get a competent professional. After you have exhausted the kitty in the cage distraction, you will need to work your dog around cats in more casual situations. This is a little trickier but it can be done. Try training, with permission of course, in your veterinarian's parking lot

Once you have your dog,s attention focused on you and off the cat, begin working sit and down stays near the cats to build Flash's self control. When this has progressed well outdoors, try it inside and finally graduate to your veterinarian's waiting room.

When you have progressed to the point that your dog will not even look at kitty on leash and will hold a stay even with the cat rubbing against him. Graduate to the same pattern of work and correction on light line, if and only if, your dog has been successfully off-leash trained.

This correction solves most all cases of cat chasing. If you honestly have thoroughly worked through this pattern of corrections to no avail, it is definitely time for a call to a qualified professional dog trainer.

CHASE GAMES FOR ATTENTION

Chase games are most often a bored dog's bid for attention. Your dog spends most of his time waiting…waiting for you to get up, waiting to be taken out, waiting to be fed, waiting for you to come home, waiting to wait! If you do not spend some quality time with your dog every day, he will invent a variety of games (often annoying) to occupy himself and to get attention from you.

Since Rascal can devote his undivided attention to studying you, he knows which objects are most important to you and when. Dogs have an excellent sense of timing. Objects are often stolen to delay your departure for work or when he sees you getting dressed up to go out. Rascal knows that if he doesn't do something quick, his opportunities for attention will soon disappear with the closing of the door. Your dog knows he will get a rise (literally) out of you if he snatches your eyeglasses when you are about to read the morning paper, the TV remote when it is time for your favorite program, or the dish towel after the dinner table has been cleared. Or, perhaps your Rascal is a petty thief that just swipes tissues and napkins, knowing you will give chase.

Of course chase games are also another symptom of lack of human leadership in Rascal's life. A dog that truly respects his human pack members would not blatantly steal and run provoking the boss's wrath! Since chase games are a result of "unemployment" and lack of respect, you must put Rascal to work with some daily obedience training. Also teach him some useful tricks, such as fetching the paper, or just some fun tricks like playing dead. (See the resource list for a tricks book).

Sufficient exercise is also a prerequisite to solving this (and many other) behavior problems. Most dogs need a minimum of a one-mile aerobic walk 5–6 days a week. An aerobic walk means keeping up a good clip without stopping so that the walk really provides heart-conditioning exercise. Also allow your Rascal some time to sniff and just do doggie things. It is a good idea to exercise your dog in the morning before you depart for the day.

Now that Rascal is on the road to reform with exercise for mind and body, chase games can be effectively corrected by using set ups with Bitter Apple and/or mouse traps such as those used for stealing. (See the chapter on Stealing).

If your dog grabs an un-booby trapped item or braves your best setup, do not chase him if at all possible (this will depend on the value of the stolen goods i.e. tissues verses eyeglasses). If he runs into a room with a door, close it. Wait 1–3 minutes (3 minutes for older dogs) and then open the door, casually. Ignore Rascal who is probably sitting, staring at the doorway, wondering why you are no longer in hot pursuit. No attention…the game no longer profitable or fun.

A six foot piece of clothesline tied to your dog's collar is an effective handle with which you can short circuit chase games. Allow your dog to trail the clothesline around the house whenever you are home. For safety reasons, remove the line when you are not home. Having Rascal drag the clothesline is especially effective on short criminals that duck under furniture (kitchen table, the bed) to avoid capture and correction.

Old-fashioned cotton clothesline is a little stiff and therefore, will not wrap around table legs creating scenes reminiscent of "The Ugliest Daschund." But any old rope you have will do. Do not use your leash. They are expensive and Rascal may take out his frustration by chewing it to pieces. Clothesline is cheap. Clothesline can also be immersed in Bitter Apple to discourage its destruction if you find yourself replacing the line frequently.

Once you have apprehended the scoundrel via the line, calmly remove the loot from his mouth by placing your hand over his muzzle, thumb on one side, fore finger on the other, and squeezing his lips between the teeth of his upper and lower jaws. Do not scold or lecture (remember attention perpetuates this behavior). Just take your possession and put Rascal on a 2–3 minute down stay. This clearly says to your dog that you have the upper hand, and you are the boss.

To end chase games, stop chasing and take control.

CHASING CARS, BICYCLES, JOGGERS, LIVESTOCK

The best prevention and the best cure for chasing cars, cyclists, joggers, livestock, and other moving things is a fenced yard. The next best deterrent is good solid off-leash training. If your dog consistently comes when called, even when faced with the most tempting distractions, when is your dog chasing cars, bicycles, joggers? OK, your situation is unique. You live on a large farm in the country, well back from the road down a long lane. Lassie is extremely well boundary-trained but tries to chew the rubber off vehicles invading her territory playing Russian roulette with her life. And when the horses play in the fields, she is chasing and nipping at their heels.

Although this problem can occur in any breed or mixture, chances are if you have a dog that is a chaser, she is a collie or other herding breed dog or mix containing herding blood. These dogs have been bred for generations to herd, that is to chase. It is important to recognize that any time we are dealing with a genetic predisposition to a trait, controlling that behavior will be more difficult. Beyond very strict training, you will need to provide an outlet for your dog's inbred drive to chase, such as regular games of ball, frisbee or agility work, if not actual herding work.

If your dog's chasing behavior is minor, relatively new, and confined to cars, bicycles joggers, or other pedestrians, you may be able to reform your dog with relatively little effort. First stop the behavior pattern by not allowing Lassie access to the targets of her pursuit when off lead. Next brush up Lassie's basic training. Remember problem solving can only be accomplished if your dog has built enough self-control to overcome the drive behind the problem behavior. On leash, work right about-turns until your dog's attention remains focused on you when the objects of her chase pass by. Then practice stays with these targets as distractions.

Now arm a helper with a squirt gun or a bottle that shoots a stream containing 1/4 white vinegar and 3/4 water. Do not use cider vinegar or a recycled bottle that may have cleaner residue, as these may irritate the eyes. At this dilution, it may sting the eyes, but will not injure them. This correction is especially useful for dogs that bark as they chase. Dogs do not like the taste of vinegar, and can quickly figure out that if they keep their mouth shut, that nasty tasting stuff can't get in there.

Have your assistant drive, ride or jog by your dog. If Lassie gives chase, have your assistant squirt her in the face repeatedly as he or she shouts "OUT!" as loud and guttural as possible. On a graph, a loud guttural "OUT!" looks as close to the graphed sound a mother dog growls when correcting her pups. You may even find it helpful if your assistant turns the table on Lassie and chases her home shouting and squirting the whole way.

Of course, do not set up your assistant for a bite. If your dog is the least bit aggressive, do not use this correction! Repeat this setup every few days with different helpers until your dog will not even think of chasing. After several setups in which your dog has shown no signs of chasing, quit setting Lassie up. A week or so later, test Lassie with a new helper. If she chases, move on to the next level of correction. It was more ingrained than you thought!

If you have a confirmed chaser of cars, bikes, people or a dog that chases livestock, reforming your dog will require a more extensive program. Once again, immediately stop the behavior pattern by not allowing Lassie access to the targets of her pursuit when off lead and brush up Lassie's basic training as outlined above. Remember Lassie must consistently obey on one command. You must not repeat commands when you correct or Lassie will not build the self-control necessary to overcome her compulsion to chase. Work until she can hold a thirty minute down stay in the face of the targets of her chase—be it cars, horses, children, etc. When your dog's on leash work is flawless, review the basic exercises off leash. Once your off-

lead control is beyond contention around all distractions *except* moving objects, it is time to go to either a thirty-foot longe line or thirty
to fifty feet of light line depending on how extreme the chasing
behavior is. You have to judge, "Can I stop Lassie when she is chasing a car full tilt by stepping on the light line or do I need to have my
hands on a good strong longe?"

Now it is time to set up the actual situations in which the problem behavior occurs. Let's use the car chaser for example and let's
assume that Lassie is extreme in this behavior. So we are going to use
the thirty-foot longe. Prearrange to have a helper drive down your
lane at a specific time. Take Lassie out near the lane five to ten minutes before the prearranged "drive by." Train Lassie for a few minutes
and then give her a release command. Allow her to relax and wander
as she pleases. Allow enough time that Lassie will be out of the working mode when the car pulls up. You ready now? Wear gloves. When
Lassie takes off after the car, step on or grab the longe line. *Do not
call your dog.* Don't say a word. Let Lassie hit the end of the lead full
tilt. Brace yourself for the jolt. Why not call her? Remember, she
already will come when called from an approaching car if your foundation is sufficient to be working this step. And we are attempting to
get Lassie to refrain from chasing cars when you are not present.
Wait a few days (she'll be more likely to fall for it again if the experience has dimmed in her memory a bit) and repeat the setup. Work
this pattern of setting Lassie up every few days until she ignores
approaching cars. Then go through the same procedure on light line.

If your dog chases more than one target you need to set her up
with all the different distractions but you do not need to exhaust one,
says cars, before you work on the other targets (horses, joggers, etc.).
In fact, this may be counter-productive. Mix it up, set Lassie up with
a car one day and a horse the next and a jogger the next. If you are
using more than one moving target, it may not be necessary to wait
few days in between setups.

If you have thoroughly worked slowly through this program and
your dog still chases, you need to have the help of a qualified professional trainer to set Lassie up with a remote controlled shock collar. A shock collar should only be used as a last resort when all other
programs have failed. Yes, it is justified. Chasing behaviors may be
life threatening to your dog in a number of ways. She may get hit by

a car, legally shot by a farmer whose livestock she is harassing, or have to be confiscated from you and euthanized if she bites a jogger or causes a pedestrian to fall or otherwise get injured.

CHEWING

Dogs chew for a variety of reasons. Puppies, not unlike human children at a certain stage, explore the world by using their mouths. This is even more essential for your canine baby since she lacks hands with which to examine her new surroundings. At approximately four and one half months, your pup will begin to teeth. Teething takes about six weeks. During this time, a pup is in twice as much pain as her human counterpart because she is both loosing her baby teeth and cutting her adult teeth. Pups will chew a variety of materials to facilitate teething. Your pup may chew wood (too often the coffee table leg) to loosen the milk teeth. Fabric (clothing and upholstery) can be worked down between teeth to massage swollen gums. Cold metal table legs help relieve the pain (ice cubes are often appreciated by your pup when gums are very sore). After teething is complete and up until a year of age, some jawbone growth takes place. Sometimes annoying to your canine adolescent, it can cause minor erratic bouts of chewing.

The final and most unfortunate cause of chewing, is that humans teach their pups, however inadvertently, to CHEW! The day you picked your little bundle of fur, you probably went to the supermarket and bought her puppy chow, new plastic bowls, a half dozen toys, and, worst of all, rawhide chewies! Every time your pup looked bored, unhappy, upset or wanted you to play, you stuck one of these objects in her mouth. The message you provided was chewing is the preferred way to relieve anxiety, boredom or just to have fun.

So let's start over from the beginning. Yes, your pup will enjoy toys, but one or two at a time is sufficient. Chewing toys should have two qualities. First, they should not be easily confused with other objects found around the house. No old socks with knots tied in them. It is true that on rare occasion, there is a dog that discriminates between her sock with the knot in it and does not generalize it as permission to chew other forms of fabric. But, this dog is the exception that proves the rule. Even more confusing than the old knotted sock toy, are rawhide chewies. You are right, Munchie loves them. Why shouldn't she? After all, rawhide is leather, hide of beef, food! Leather with human scent on is even better! WOW! Shoes, gloves, furniture and even Naugahyde will do in a pinch. Besides developing a taste for leather, rawhide chewies do not always completely digest as the manufacturers would have you believe. They can cause intestinal blockages, which can be serious enough to require surgery.

The second quality a chewing toy should have is indestructibility. Dogs shred the flesh of their kill to eat in the wild. Since the natural wild instincts are just under the surface of those big brown eyes, dogs quickly learn the joy of shredding newspaper, magazines, carpet, squeaky toys, etc. Squeaky toys are OK provided your dog does not destroy them. If you find yourself replacing them every week at the supermarket, stop. Besides, those little squeakies are rough on the digestive tract if swallowed.

OK, now that I have told you a lot of money was wasted on unacceptable chewing toys, what can your dog have? Your dog can have a Nylabone or its softer (for puppies) counterpart, a Gumabone. These name brand products that come in various sizes and shapes are made of hard, solid nylon. You say you bought a Nylabone and Munchie will not touch it? This is often the case until the ends get roughed up. So try a little grease on the ends to get her started. This is usually not a problem with the Gumabone version. Nylabones and Gumabones are not confusing (not too many hard nylon objects lying around my house) and are indestructible.

Your pup may also have a solid rubber ball. Please get one large enough so it cannot roll down your dog's throat and choke her. Do not get the kind with the bell inside since the hole gives the dog a spot from which to destroy the ball. These balls are expensive but, unless lost, will last for years and can provide you and your dog hours of enjoyment playing fetch as well as serving as a chew toy. Other rubber toys such as bone shaped ones can easily be chewed up. Tug toys are a bad idea all the way around. Besides tug toys being easily chewed up, tugging may cause aggression problems in some dogs.

An inexpensive canine favorite is the "Natural bone." Available in pet shops, it is a portion of beef shank bone that has been processed to make very hard and non-splintering.

The final and ultimate chewing object is the knuckle bone (soup bone). You must prepare these bones yourself. Raw, the knuckle bone will not splinter like the shank portion of a bone. But, to be on the safe side, knuckle bones should be prepared according to the following recipe:

> 3–4 LARGE WHOLE knuckle bones (should be at least the size of a softball).
> Cover with water and add 1/4 cup vinegar (garlic and onions help hide the odor and dogs like the taste).
> Cover and simmer for 2–4 hours.
> Drain, cool, and clean off excess fat and gristle.
> Freeze (zip loc bags work nicely)

Knuckle bones have a specific use in our anti chewing program. More on their use later.

Now that you have disposed of all those bad chewing toys and have purchased acceptable ones, what do you do with them? In the beginning, with a very young pup, you can trade a forbidden object with one of these toys. For example, your pup has picked up your underwear, tell her "NO" and take it away, offering the pup one of her toys. While we are on the subject, there is nothing like a pup to teach children and adults to put dirty clothes in the hamper and shoes in the closet.

Chew toys can also be used occasionally to pacify your pup when you are busy, or for play time. However, do not rely on toys to occupy most of her time. Your pup needs you to spend time with her! Take her outside for a walk or for a game of fetch. Regular exercise is a must, not only for health, but also to prevent or resolve behavior problems.

OK so you did it all right (including starting your pup in basic obedience training) and now your pup is teething and she has expanded her toy selection to include yours. What to do? Well, you have provided your pup with acceptable toys and you are using a cage for housebreaking purposes. The time your pup is loose in the house is supervised so she has not had a chance for real destruction. But, her attempts are leaving scars on the table legs and you with crotchless underwear! The answer is Grannick's Bitter Apple or Sour Grapes manufactured by Vo-Toys, Inc. I am expressly naming these two no-chew products because they work the best. Many others on the market smell bad and are ineffective.

To correct a chewing problem with Bitter Apple (or Sour Grapes), your dog must be set up. We do not want your dog to learn not to chew when she sees you spraying or when target objects smell like alcohol (base for Bitter Apple and Sour Grapes). We want to affect a lifetime cure so you can stop spraying things with a no-chew product. To set your dog up, put her outside (if the yard is fenced) or have someone take her for a walk. Mist a few target objects (an already ruined pair of underwear, a newspaper, the corner of the carpet or whatever your pup fancies) lightly with the no-chew product. Doggie-proof the rest of the area by placing untreated items out of reach. Wait ten minutes before letting your dog come into the area. Although Bitter Apple and Sour Grapes have no offensive odor, their alcohol base can be detected shortly after spraying, especially by hunting breeds.

The beauty of this correction is that it will work whether or not you are present and involves no negative exchange between you and your dog. She picks up that treated pair of underwear and it tastes bad, so she spits it out and gets one of her own toys. This correction requires no violent confrontation between you and your dog. Scolding often feeds a chewing problem. Remember, one of the common reasons dogs chew is boredom or to get attention. Your past confrontations broke the boredom and got your dog your attention! Like children, dogs will work for negative attention if that is all that is available. To your dog, negative attention is better than no attention at all.

A few notes on the use of Bitter Apple. It evaporates in a few of hours. Therefore, if you are working on this problem throughout the day, it will require several sprayings. However, if you have a working household, one spraying when you return home from work may do it. Some dogs (less than 20%) will chew in spite of Bitter Apple—try

Sour Grapes. Please test a spot before spraying either product on expensive upholstery or fabric. If it isn't color fast, you can loosely tack a piece of old sheet or other fabric over that area and spray it. Finally, in order to effect a cure, Bitter Apple must be consistently used for at least two weeks running (the length of the critical learn period in dogs). Often, dogs make a couple attempts on treated objects and don't try again for a few days. If you rake this as a clue to stop spraying, she will sure enough try it again a week later and you will have to start all over!

At about six to eight months of age, your pup will be ready to start weaning out of her cage. As discussed in the house training program, you will first leave her loose at night in your bedroom or another single room. If any chewing takes place, set her up with Bitter Apple just prior to bedtime. When she has proven herself responsible overnight, it is time to leave her for short periods during the day gradually building up to the necessary length of time required by your schedule.

What about those older dogs or adolescents that only chew while you are away? First of all, you are not alone; this is the most common chewing situation. It's boring and lonely when you're not home. Remember, you are your loving pet's reason for living! As discussed in the housebreaking chapter, leaving your dog outside in a fenced yard or dog kennel (pen) during the day is ideal, but sometimes not possible. So, just before leaving for work, doggie proof the area to which your dog has access and set her up with Bitter Apple. DO NOT say a big goodbye (or hello when you return). This builds up anxiety. Just leave, but as you do, pull one of those knuckle bones out of the freezer and toss it to your dog. Now, instead of your departure being a buildup of anxiety, you have simply left and she has a wonderful treat with which to occupy herself. Observations have shown that most destructive chewing takes place within the first thirty minutes after you leave—when emotions are high. OK, we've gotten her through that much, now she hears a noise outside and goes to the window to investigate. On the way back, a magazine jumps into her mouth! But what's this? It tastes terrible (like Bitter Apple) and she returns to her knuckle bone.

If your dog manages to chew something left untreated, DO NOT SCOLD HER!! It's difficult but you must hold your tongue. Remember, with chewing problems, negative attention often feeds the behavior. Frequently clients make the comment, "Munchie knows when she does something wrong because she hides when I get home." With an occasional canine genius, this may be true. However dogs live mostly in the present moment. At the time your dog was engaged in destructive chewing, it was not unpleasant. More often, Munchie hides when you return home because you are often incomprehensibly angry, from your dog's point of view. This is especially true if your corrections have been so severe that your dog was too frightened to make the connection between your anger and her unacceptable deed.

As in housebreaking, a high quality diet is essential in preventing problems. Occasionally, a dog on the best of diets will suffer form a mineral deficiency. Characteristic behaviors of a mineral deficient dog are voracious chewing and eating part or all of what is chewed. A classic symptom is chewing and eating wallboard because of its mineral content. Mineral deficient dogs also like wood, plants, soil, rocks, book bindings, and carpet backing (because of the minerals in the glue). Mineral deficient dogs are also prone to hyperactivity. No amount of correction will stop a mineral deficient dog from chewing because their bodies are craving what is missing from their diet.

To correct a mineral deficiency, get a human organic multi-mineral supplement—<u>NOT</u> a vitamin and mineral supplement, just minerals. Try a health food store. Give a medium sized dog (65 pounds) half the adult minimum dose. It takes about two to three weeks for the mineral supplement to have an effect. In the meantime, you'll have to depend on environmental engineering (put the dog outside or in her cage when you are not home) to prevent destruction. After two to three weeks on the supplement, you will see a drastic decrease in chewing. Often there is a residual minor chewing habit to be correct. Now the previous outlined programs will be effective in completely ending this behavior.

This program has repeatedly been successful for my clients, even for reforming chewers with which many other corrections have failed. Very rarely, but it does happen, there are some dogs that persist in chewing. There are more severe corrections but should only be applied under the direction of a qualified trainer.

Note: <u>Pica</u>, the behavior of swallowing whole a variety of objects, is not a chewing problem. This behavior is most often seen in Dalmatians. Although some of the procedure outlined here for chewing, may also apply to the dog suffering form Pica, more extensive correction may be required. Please contact a qualified trainer or a behaviorist veterinarian for assistance.

COURTESY AT THE DOOR

Courtesy at the door, in its final form, means that your dog voluntarily sits and stay while you open the door to have company enter or for you to pass through the doorway ahead of your dog. This behavior eliminates door bolting for escape as well as overly excited greeting of company. So it serves two purposes, good manners and safety.

Teaching courtesy at the door requires your dog to have a solid three minute sit-stay that has been thoroughly distraction-proofed. Once that has been accomplished you are ready to proceed with using that training in the problem area, the doorway. However, first you and your family must agree on at which doors you will teach and enforce the exercise. You may not want to teach courtesy at the door at every door to your home. The essential doors to teach this behavior at are those through which visitors enter your house, for good manners, and those that open into unfenced areas, for safety. For example, you may not wish to teach courtesy at the door at the backdoor that opens into your dog's yard and through which guests do not enter your home.

To teach courtesy at the door (this is the name of the exercise, there is no command "courtesy at the door") start with your dog **on leash** and have her sit and stay back far enough from the door that you can open it fully. Practice several stays with you opening the door until your dog no longer breaks the stay. Now place your dog on a sit-stay, open the door and you pass through the doorway. If your dog breaks her stay when you proceed through the door, correct the broken stay. If your dog has been properly trained with a left foot signal to heel, make sure you are leading off your your right foot. Repeat this step until you can exit and your dog holds her stay. Next step is to give your dog her release command (the word or phrase that releases your dog from a command) after you have started through the doorway, so she may go out <u>BEHIND</u> you if it is your desire to have your dog exit also. **Now put your dog on a sit-stay on the other side of the doorway.** After she has briefly held the second stay, release your dog and go on to whatever you went outside for.

When returning indoors, follow the same series. Have your dog hold a sit-stay before you open the door, release her to <u>follow </u>you in, and have her hold a sit-stay inside the door. So there is a sit-stay, **before** and **after** the door way in both directions, entering and exiting. Often handlers skip the stay after the doorway. This greatly decreases the effectiveness and usefulness of courtesy at the door. If your dog is not made to hold a stay after passing through the door way going out into an unfenced area, she make bolt into the path of a noisy delivery truck never hearing your command to come and be hurt or killed! Not having your dog hold a sit-stay after the door decreases the effectiveness of courtesy at the door, even if it does not endanger her well being, because dogs respond to the consistency of the pattern: sit-stay before the doorway, passage through the doorway, sit-stay after passing through the doorway both entering and exiting.

<u>EVERYONE</u> in your household must enforce courtesy at the door <u>EVERY TIME </u>you answer the door or take your dog out. After this has been done consistently for two weeks (a critical learning period for a dog), demand that your dog perform the sit-stays <u>without</u> being told! If your dog does not automatically sit and stay without being told, correct her just as if you had given the verbal commands. Even before the two weeks of teaching courtesy at the door was completed, you probably experienced occasions where your dog sat before you had a chance to tell her. Teach it for two weeks with verbal commands anyhow to make sure there is no confusion before you progress to automatic stays.

Now the behavior of courtesy at the door is being initiated by the doorway and not the handler. This is another reason that everyone enforcing courtesy at the door is critical for your dog to comprehend completely what is expected of her. Having the behavior triggered by the door way and *not* a handler is essential if you wish your dog to stay safely inside your house when no one is present and the door blows open or the kids leave it ajar. One of my own dogs set a personal record waiting inside an open door for over two hours while home alone! I know because my very "observant" neighbor, came over exclaiming as I returned home that Buster had been laying inside the open doorway since shortly after I had departed. The neighbor knew better than to try and shut the door since Buster was a trained guard dog. It was doubly fortunate that Buster's courtesy at the door was solid because he was an Akita, and may have snacked on a few little four legged tender morsels in the neighborhood had he ventured out.

This is how courtesy at the door looks at this stage. You approach the door(s) with your dog on leash and she voluntarily sits and stays while you open the door and proceed through. Upon your release command, your dog follows you through the doorway and voluntarily sits and stays on the other side of the door. She does this both exiting and entering your home through the chosen doorways. Even though the stays are automatic, you must always give your dog a verbal release command to allow her to proceed through the door. There may be situations where you do not want her to follow you in or out or you are answering the door to have company come in and neither of you is exiting.

OK, you have thoroughly taught courtesy at the door, and your dog has improved tremendously but is still a problem when company calls? Rehearse it! A few rehearsals of a problem situations with a well-trained dog usually ends the problem. Get a helper, which can be a family member to start with, to arrive at an appointed time, say 2:00 PM, and knock on your door. At 1:55 PM, put your dog on leash and practice her basic obedience commands (heel, sit, stay, down and come) inside your house. Now your dog is in working mode. When the knock sounds, heel your dog to the door. If she breaks the heel and pulls toward the door, correct her. Then put your dog on a sit-stay at the door (remember to place her far enough back that the door can be opened fully). Tell your helper to open the door. (It is better for your helper to handle the door so you have both hands available to handle your dog.) If your dog breaks her stay when the door opens, you correct the broken stay and your helper should back out the door shutting it as he or she goes. Try again starting with your helper knocking. Repeat this pattern until your helper can open the door without your dog breaking the stay. Then have your helper enter your house. If your dog breaks her stay at this point, your helper should back out, shutting the door as he or she goes. Repeat this phase until there is no contention. Next have your helper pet your dog. If your dog breaks at this point, have your helper back up one step. Your helper need not go back outside unless your dog becomes very excited. Repeat until your helper can pet your dog without her breaking the stay. Now heel your dog to the nearest chair put her on a down-stay near you so you can easily correct if she breaks and both you and your helper have a seat!

I know it sounds like a lot when you read the procedure but it probably took longer to type it then the whole exercise took you and your helper to perform if your dog was properly trained prior to the rehearsal. If not shame on you. After a couple of rehearsals with family members, your dog' should be performing courtesy at the door flawlessly. Now rehearse once more *without* training your dog just before your helper knocks. A more realistic set up. Have your dog's leash hanging on the door knob, so you can snap it on her when you hear the knock. Proceed as before. Once your dog is good at this level, try a rehearsal with someone other than a family member that can follow instructions. Keep the leash hanging on the door knob so that you can snap it on your dog quickly for all those unplanned situations as well as when your are practicing.

Once your dog is consistently good at her door manners on leash enforce them without the leash being on but have it handy in case your dog backslides. Of course your dog has to have been thoroughly off-leash trained if you expect her to obey in exciting situations like company arriving without having her leash on.

If after all your efforts in thoroughly teaching and training courtesy at the door, Flash still occasionally bolts outside when the door is opened, here's the cure. Get a ten foot piece of cotton clothesline and at one end tie a knot large enough that it will catch in between the door and frame when the door is shut on the line. Allow Flash to trail the line around the house all the time a human is present. If when you open the door, Flash bolts, slam the door shut on the clothesline. When the knot catches in the door frame, Flash will give herself such a sound correction that she will think twice before bolting the door again. How set your dog is in this bolting behavior will determine how long she must wear the knotted clothesline. You may also have a helper open the door from the outside and slam it shut on the line. Needless to say this requires some coordination and timing on the humans part. If you are slow, use a longer piece of clothesline. This set up is rarely needed if courtesy at the door has been properly taught and enforced.

CROTCH SNIFFING

This topic always brings to mind a bawdy little cartoon of a mother dog scolding her pup saying, "Now Junior, mind your manners and sniff Mrs. Johnson's…Mrs. Johnson was another dog, of course. We humans tend to find this ritual of canine greeting a little offensive.

Crotch sniffing is easily corrected by doing formal introductions with your dog and his potential victims whether meeting people on the street or in your home. Put your dog **on leash** on a sit-stay when someone approaches. If he breaks the stay, correct. Correct any attempts at sniffing with a stay correction also. If the introductee is a guest in your home, put Junior on a down-stay after the introduction to prevent any farther attempts at accosting your company. After he is quite calm, release him from the stay. Allow him to be on his own time as long as he is using good manners. If he acts up, put him on another down-stay.

If you are Junior's object of affection, command him to sit every time he approaches you. Give the command well enough in advance that Junior is sitting before his nose is in your crotch. Having him trail a leash, six feet of rope or wear a tab, if you are that advanced in his obedience training, makes correction much easier. And what about that sneak-up-and-get-you-from-behind sniffer? Definitely have him trail a leash or line so you can step on it to prevent his escape as you blast him with a solution of 1/4 white vinegar and 3/4 water from a squirt gun right in the offending nose!

Most often this is a behavior of intact male dogs. Have your dog neutered! Neutering prevents health and behavior problems as well as unwanted puppies. You say you want to breed Junior? Are you a qualified breeder? One who is a student of genetics and pedigrees? If not, you may be doing your breed a great disservice as well as the pups you would breed and the purchasers of those pups, not to mention the five million homeless dogs killed each year.

DIGGING HOLES IN THE YARD

Dogs dig holes in the ground to follow prey and for the sheer joy of it. They also dig to make a cool hole in which to lie. In the wild, dogs dig dens in the ground to provide shelter for whelping (giving birth) and rearing their pups. Dogs dig is to bury food stores. Some escape artist dig under fences. Certain breeds are more prone to digging because of their genetics. If you purchase a terrier, you must accept a certain amount of digging—possibly a large amount. Terrier is from the Latin "terra" which means earth. Terriers have been bred to go to ground for hundreds of years. There are some breeds of terriers that people don't generally recognize as such. The old German black and tan terrier was used to develop the Doberman Pinscher (Pinscher in German means terrier).

In analyzing their motives, we can see some routes to prevention and resolution of the problem. If you have moles or gofers in your yard, you must get rid of them to stop the trenching. Use mole traps or treat the yard for grubs. The moles will vacate your premises if their food source is depleted. Do not use mole bait. Not only will it poison the moles, but it will poison your dog as well! Cats also work nicely for nontoxic mole extermination, and there are many cats disparately in need of homes. If your dog is digging to bury bones or toys, stop allowing him to have toys outside. If your dog is digging holes to make a cool resting place, please allow one or two in a area that is out of the way. Do not tie your dog outside for longer than five minutes. Chaining dogs up is cruel. It causes digging, barking, and often aggression problems. Do not let your excavator watch you dig in the earth. Dogs can learn by mimicking. Gardening should be done without canine companionship if your dog has a digging problem. If your dog digs for the sheer joy of feeling fresh earth fly under foot, frequent nail clipping will discourage excavation. Use a guillotine type nail clipper so you can slice off a sliver of nail every few days. By keeping the quick, which contains a nerve besides a blood vessel, exposed, it is uncomfortable to dig after a few strokes.

I don't know what they do with all the dirt, but there is seldom enough to refill the holes. Adding some of your dog's stool will repel some clean dogs from digging. Moth flakes are the best dog repellent. Naphthalene is the active ingredient in moth balls, crystals and flakes, as well as many commercially produced dog repellents. The garden center products cost and arm and a leg for mostly filler! You have your own filler—mulch and dirt. Naphthalene is **poisonous**, so do not use moth balls. Your pup may wolf down three or four white marbles before getting a snout full of their scent making him sick. Moth flakes are ground up, and mixed with mulch or dirt, your dog will smell them before eating any. Moth flakes can be mixed in mulch in flower beds or dirt in that hole by the back step to repel your dog from specific areas.

There are two effective methods of thwarting the canine escape artist. You can line the inside of your fence within an 18" wide strip of fencing laid on the ground. Remove your sod or dig down two to three inches in the ground and lay the strip of fencing on the ground and stake it down. Also attach the strip to the fence. Replace your sod or cover the strip with soil. When your dog digs, he'll hit the buried wire and stop. Dogs never seem to figure out to back up a couple of feet and tunnel under the whole arrangement.

Another extremely effective way to stop digging under the fence is to use an electric fence charge. Now don't gasp. I am not talking about the voltage that keeps in cattle. There are fence chargers designed to keep pests such as dogs and rabbits out of gardens that only charge 6–8 volts. It will scare a dog or child but will not injure either one. Run an electric fence wire around the bottom of the inside of your fence. The insulators can be attached to your fence posts or be placed on plant stakes a foot inside the fence. Leave the wire charged for one month. Then you should be able to turn it off, but leave the wire up for at least another month. A note for success— fence chargers must be well grounded to work properly.

A last-resort correction is a modification of the "water in the hole torture." If you have <u>tried everything else</u> and you must stop the digging or get rid of your dog, catch Dozer in the act of digging a hole. Scold her firmly while tracing a line from her eye to the hole. Then make Dozer hold a ten to twenty minute down stay at the scene of the crime. After you release Dozer from the stay, do not allow her to make up to you for the rest of the day.

DIGGING IN FURNITURE, CARPETS, AND WALLS

Dogs dig in furniture, carpets, and walls for several reasons. Often dogs dig in furniture or rugs to make a nest. Sometimes their digging is an attempt to get to or bury something. There may be a lost toy in the crevices of the couch or a lost piece of popcorn! Or Digger may be attempting to hide a toy or dog treat. Dogs often smell the scent of spilled food on furniture and carpet and dig to get to the "buried treasure." Sometimes they smell a mouse under the floor boards or in a wall. Dogs also dig at walls because of a mineral deficiency.

If your dog is digging in the furniture, thoroughly vacuum and clean the furniture, making sure there are no hidden treasures or enticing scents. Do not give your dog treats if he is burying them in the furniture unless you are going to supervise him with the treat until it is eaten. If cleaning doesn't solve the problem, banish Digger from the furniture. See the chapter on "Climbing On The Furniture" for the proper way to teach your dog that she is no longer allowed on the furniture.

If your dog is digging in carpets, thoroughly clean them to remove any food scents. Check your house for signs of rodents and take the necessary steps to rid your home of pests if they are present. Often this behavior started because there was some enticing scent in or under the carpet and it becomes a habit even after the scent is removed. Sometimes the habit pattern can be broken by simply moving a piece of furniture over the excavation site for about two weeks. If it is not possible to rearrange the furniture there are several other things you can try. One is a dog repellent. Unfortunately, most dog repellents stink. The most effective repellent is good old fashioned moth flakes. Moth flakes are **poisonous** and must be used with caution! Farnum makes an indoor dog repellent called B'Have that I have used with some success.

Fortunately, dogs usually pick one or two favorite spots in which to dig. So you can also try a scat mat on Digger's chosen spots. Although I am not a big fan of training gimmicks, I like to experiment with new products in hopes of finding something really useful. Of course, I do this on my own animals before recommending a product to a client. At my wits end as to how to stop my cat from aggravating a neighbor by walking on the hood of his car leaving little kitty foot prints, I purchased a scat mat . The scat mat shocks the offending dog or cat when it touches the mat. These devices are effective as long as they are in place. So my cat learned not to walk on the neighbors car for as long as he used the scat mat which wasn't very long. At least I had given my neighbor a viable solution and he did not complain any more even though the cat continued to get on his car when he forgot to put the mat in place.

If your dog is scratching and digging at the walls of your home, you probably have a mouse or some other pest in residence. Check it out thoroughly. It can happen in the best of homes, even brand new ones. If there are no pests in the walls, consider a mineral deficiency. Your dog may be digging at the walls to eat the wall board. Occasionally, a dog on the best of diets will suffer from a mineral deficiency. Characteristic behaviors of these dogs are voracious chewers that eat part or all of what they chew. A classic symptom is chewing and eating wallboard because of its mineral content. Mineral deficient dogs also like wood, plants, soil, rocks, book bindings, and carpet backing (because of the minerals in the glue). No amount of correction will stop a mineral-deficient dog form digging, chewing, and eating a strange variety of things because their bodies are craving what is missing from their diet.

To correct a mineral deficiency, get a human organic multi-mineral supplement—<u>not</u> a vitamin and mineral supplement, just minerals. Try a health food store. Give a medium-sized dog (65 pounds) half the adult human dose. It takes about two to three weeks for the minerals to have an effect. In the meantime, you'll have to depend on environmental engineering to prevent destruction. Put the dog outside or in her cage when you are not home. After two to three weeks on the supplement, you will see a drastic decrease in the crave-driven behaviors. Often, there is a residual minor digging or chewing problem to correct. Now the previous outlined programs will be effective in completely ending these behaviors.

DOG AGGRESSION

Dog aggression can range from leash pulling to investigate another dog to full-blown attempts at "dog slaughter." Dog aggression can be as deeply rooted as genetics, or it may simply be a matter of lack of socialization as a pup. It may be the result a traumatic event such as an attack by another dog, the jealousy or over-protectiveness for an owner or territory, or it may be evidence of just plain dominance. Sometimes aggression starts with age. Two things can happen simultaneously as a dog ages. The older dog becomes grumpy because of pain of arthritis or some other failing and a younger dog begins to challenge the aging dog for pack leadership.

Outside of the home, the most common form of dog aggression is lunging at another dog when walking on a leash. This may start simply as curiosity about a fellow of the species and snowball into aggression. Territoriality, jealousy, protectiveness, breeding and natural dominance as well as pain may all contribute to the progression from curiosity to aggression. When your dog is pulling on the leash, it is causing pain in his or her neck that becomes associated with the object of the dog's attention—this case another dog. Whatever the combination of causes, the solution is the same, properly executed right-about turns. Starting far enough away from another dog so that you can correct effectively, begin making right about turns and continue until your dog is no longer distracted by the other dog at that distance. Now move in a little closer and again work right-about turns until your dog is watching you and not the other dog. Continue to work in this pattern until you can walk by another dog without your dog taking his or her eyes off you. When you begin this process it is best to arrange to have your distraction, another dog, appear in an area where you have plenty of room to work. As your control and Rambo's manners improve, move on to more casual situations. Do not forget about your veterinarian's parking lot as a treasure trove of distractions. Ask permission to train there first!

When you and Rambo have achieved the goal of being able to walk past another dog, start having him or her hold stays in the presence of other dogs to continue to build his or her self control. Work around other dogs daily for two weeks and you shall have reformed Rambo to the point that he or she no longer lunges at other dogs and can hold a stay in the company of another dog. If you feel you cannot do this, you need to seek out qualified professional help. I might add at this point that some aggressive dogs can only be reformed to the point of being controllable in the presence of other dogs. Some dogs just do not like other dogs and although we can demand good behavior in their presence, we can not always make Rambo love his fellow dog. Aggressive dogs should not be off-leash in any area they may encounter another dog.

IF A DOG FIGHT OCCURS, NEVER REACH FOR A DOG'S COLLAR!

Any fighting dog may bite you and not even realize it was a human. There are several ways to break up a fight. Outdoors, turn a cold water hose on feuding dogs. Blast them hard in their faces. You can shove a board, trash can lid or a shovel in between them. If two people are present, on the count of three, each grab the hind legs of one dog and yank hard simultaneously. Hopefully you will knock the dogs down on their chests and the wind out of them. If you cannot intervene safely DON'T! Let them fight. Dog bites can be serious injuries and they almost always get infected. Occasionally an enraged dog will turn on a human in the frenzy of a fight. Then you have the potential to receive multiple serious wounds!!!

If you have read the chapter on introducing a second dog into your home, you know that I generally do not recommend more than one dog per household for a variety of reasons, one of which is dog fighting. A single dog forms his or her pack with the humans in the home, a mixed pack. Two dogs, depending on the temperament and age each was acquired, may be more or less bonded to each other and the humans in the household. With three or more dogs in one home, the dogs will begin to form a true dog pack exclusive of the humans present. Pack behavior greatly changes the behavior of the individual. If the pack members are not well balanced, some dog is going to be the odd one out. The others may gang up on it. The resulting dog fights are potentially disastrous. Not only may the dogs be injured or one killed, but humans often get bitten trying to break up fights. There is also emotional damage done to four leggeds as well as the two leggeds when the solution becomes to get rid of one or more of the dogs. Very often children suffer in this situation. Not only is there the potential for a serious physical injury, but there is the possibility of heartbreak if a child must part with a beloved friend. So DO NOT set yourself, your family, or any innocent dogs up in this potential misfortune.

If fighting suddenly breaks out among dogs that have formerly gotten along well, have each dog checked for possible health problems. Sometimes extreme stress in a home (death of a loved one, illness, divorce) can initiate fighting among the canine family members. This aggression may become habitual and not spontaneously disappear when the stress decreases. Intervene when it starts. Don't wait until it escalates to real blood.

Often when two dogs from one home are separated for a while, they fight when reunited. Be aware of the possibility and reintroduce your dogs in a neutral territory (not your living room). Immediately intervene if any grumbling starts. Don't leave the dogs home alone together until your are sure they have rekindled their friendship.

If you already have a multi-dog household and are in the middle of civil war, you must be a strong pack leader with solid control over your dogs to have any hope of resolving the dog aggression problem. You bet—back to the foundation of basic obedience training in which your dogs learn to consistently respond on one command in distracting situations. If the dogs in your home recognize you are the big boss and you make it clear to them that fighting is not allowed, peace may reign. How do you make it clear to Hatfield and McCoy that there will be no feudin' on your territory? When even the slightest grumbling starts, all dogs go on down stays. If there is any growling on the stays, squirt the offending dog(s) in the mouth with 1/4 white vinegar and 3/4 water from a spray bottle that shoots a strong stream.

If the dog being squirted (or any other) breaks the stay, correct the broken stays.

Remove any bones of contention. If your dogs fight over toys, no toys until they can behave themselves. If they fight over food, either feed them in separate rooms or at opposite ends of one room with you supervising in the middle. The latter is preferred since separating when feeding may build contention resulting in a fight when the dogs are reunited. If your dogs fight over you or other family members, give each dog quality time in the form of daily training and exercise individually and in the presence of each other with one handler for each dog. Handlers should frequently switch dogs (the same person should not always train the same dog).

This problem can take a while to resolve. Do not leave Hatfield and McCoy alone together until there has been no aggression for several weeks. If after a month of serious work on your part you have not resolved the fighting or if at any point it escalates, seek the help of a qualified professional trainer. Unfortunately, very often the solution is to place one of the dogs in another home.

FEAR OF THUNDER STORMS AND LOUD NOISES

Fear of thunder storms and other loud noises such as firecrackers and gunfire is a common phobia in dogs. It is natural for an animal to become restless wanting to seek shelter when a storm is approaching because of the possible danger. Sometimes the natural survival instinct runs amuck and a dog will become so fearful during storms that he will destroy property and injure himself. Noise phobia may also be triggered by a terrifying experience associated with a loud noise. Having a firecracker explode near a dog can cause noise phobia. I had a dog who became afraid of storms and loud noises after a tray of glasses was dropped and shattered on the floor right behind her. Gun shyness is usually caused by the inept use of a gun—for example, shooting over a dog and peppering her with shot, or exposing a pup that is too young to gunshot. Ordinarily, dogs are more easily traumatized when young, but it can happen at any age. One dog in a household that is afraid of storms or noises will teach another dog this fear. Moreover, humans that are afraid of storms will instill their fear in their dogs. I have known of dogs so fearful of storms that they have jumped out second story windows, clawed holes in walls, and chewed through cages and chain link fences in their panic. The German Shepherd Dog is the breed most prone to becoming phobic of loud noises because they have very sensitive hearing. However, this problem can occur in any breed or mix.

If you having a budding noise phobia in your dog, you may be able to stop the fear progression before your dog becomes destructive to your home or herself. When this problem is in its infancy, the dog will become slightly agitated as a storm approaches (or during hunting season when there is a lot of gun fire, or when there are fireworks set off in the area). Often the dog will sense the storm before you. They are responding to the change in barometric pressure even before the storm is audible. Pay attention! Your dog will seek you out for comfort. DO NOT pet the dog soothingly and coo to her that everything will be OK. If you do, you will reenforce your dog's irrational nervous behavior. The timing of praise or correction is critical. You must praise or correct according to what the dog is **thinking** (not necessarily what she is physically doing). If your dog is thinking the sky is going to fall in and "I am going to die," and you are petting and talking soothingly to your dog, you are praising those neurotic thoughts.

Of course, the prevention and solution to this problem lies largely in sound obedience training. When your dog seeks you out for reassurance at the approach of a storm, put her on a down-stay! This requires her to use self control and will help her calm herself down. Nervousness is not an excuse for breaking the stay. Correct a broken stay as you would in any other situation. Once your dog seems to be back in control of herself, release her from the stay and praise her for it. If your dog becomes agitated when released from the stay, put her on another. By using stays you are providing your dog with security in your authority as a pack leader and giving her something to think about instead of panicking.

TTouch (see the chapter of that name) is also of value is resolving fear of storms. You need to practice TTouch regularly on your dog when it is not storming. Regular practice trains the mind and body to unconsciously respond to the TTouch. For example, the next time you get in the dentist's chair, take inventory of your body. Most likely you have tensed up. Or conversely, if you take massage regularly, your body will begin to relax as soon as you lay on the table even before the therapist puts a hand on you. This kind of unconscious response greatly facilitates relaxation in your nervous dog during a storm, or in the vicinity of other loud noises. The combination of a down stay and TTouch is very effective in relieving anxiety and allowing your dog to learn that she has nothing to fear.

You will need a strong cage to confine your dog to when storms are eminent and you must be away from home. The cage should be just big enough for your dog to stand, turn around, and lie down comfortably. If a cage is too big, it will not provide your dog with the secure feeling of a den and the extra space will give her room to work herself up into a panic. Sometimes covering the cage with a blanket so it feels even more den-like to your dog helps, as long as your dog will not get overheated.

If your dog is untrained and has progressed to the point of being destructive to your home and herself, you may need to use an anxiety relieving drug until you have the dog solidly trained and can begin the behavior modification program outlined above. Please avoid the use of tranquilizers if at all possible because they interfere with your dog's learning processes. Drugs are not a good longterm solution and even in the short term, are of limited value, you cannot always predict the approach of a storm well enough in advance to have your dog under the influence before the storm arrives and she panics.

As in all things, an ounce of prevention is worth a pound of cure. Bring your dog indoors if someone is setting off firecrackers in your neighborhood; only allow an expert gun person to shoot over your dog; do not allow your dog to associate with another that is fearful during storms; and do not feed into your dogs natural agitation at the approach of storms!

CLIMBING ON THE FURNITURE

Climbing on the furniture, unfortunately, is often taught to young pups by their owners. Holding a pup on your lap while you are sitting on the couch teaches your pup he is allowed up on the furniture. Since pups tend to see things as either black or white, on the furniture on a human's lap, is the same as on the furniture without human invitation. If you do not want your pup on furniture, only hold your pup on your lap when you are sitting on the floor.

Allowing your dog on the furniture or not is your preference. However, I want to point out a few possible problems. Dogs can track up dirt and fleas. With some dogs, allowing them on the furniture might cause confusion in the pack order. In a wild dog pack, the leader picks the most choice place to sleep, food to eat and so forth. Translation to the mixed human/dog pack is that humans (leaders) get on the furniture and dogs (followers) belong on the floor. Even if you decide to allow your dog on the furniture, he should not be allowed on your bed. Allowing your dog on your bed obviously elevates your dog to your level demoting you from pack leader.

Often, dog owners try to teach their pups that they are allowed on one piece of furniture, but not others. This sometimes works with some dogs that have an above average ability to discriminate and a high desire to please their masters. But with most pups, it's all or nothing, black or white, furniture or no furniture. Even with the exceptional pup, it is harder to teach the distinction between furniture on which they are permitted and that which is forbidden. Therefore, your run the risk of creating unnecessary confusion.

Once the problem of climbing on the furniture exists, you have to be honest about whether you taught the behavior to your pup. If dealing with a "secondhand" dog, was it allowed on the furniture in his prior home? If so, you must first teach the dog that this behavior is no longer permissible. It is unfair to correct a dog if he does not understand what he is doing wrong. After all, you are the one changing the rules.

To teach your dog that he is not allowed on the furniture, tell him "OFF!", (not "down", that is an obedience command) and gently pull the dog to the floor. Place your dog on a one to two minute down-stay right in front of the furniture. This clearly shows a dog, in a way he can understand, that he belongs on the floor, not on the furniture. You must do this for two weeks <u>every</u> time your dog hops up on any piece of furniture. (On the average, dogs have a critical learning period of two weeks. Therefore, it takes approximately two weeks to break a habit or teach a behavior.)

When you have consistently taught your dog the new rule for two weeks running, you can add correction. Now when your dog hops up onto the furniture tell him "OFF!" and <u>jerk</u> him to the floor. Follow up with a down-stay to reinforce where your dog belongs and to make him think over what he did wrong.

Sometimes, providing your pet with is own dog bed can help prevent or speed up the resolution of the dog-on-the-furniture problem. However, a dog bed is a privilege that should be earned. Your pup should be a year old and passed any attempt to chew and not be showing any signs of possessive aggression (growling over food, toys, climbing off the furniture, etc.) Do not purchase a wicker bed. More dogs chew wicker than any other type of dog bed. A cedar and foam filled bed will do nicely. The cedar repels fleas. My old dog's favorite is a bean bag chair. Make sure the bed you choose has a removable, washable cover.

Often, a dog learns that his owner does not appreciate his being on the furniture and also realizes that he can get away with it when his master is not home. Mouse traps will correct the canine sneak. Place set mouse traps on the furniture spaced so the dog cannot hop up without setting one off. Cover the traps with a tissue to disguise them. If your dog is likely to swipe the tissue, spray it with Grannick's Bitter Apple (an effective canine anti-chew product available in most pet shops). Of course, <u>do not</u> let your dog see you set him up.

If you do not want to fool with the mouse traps or fear your cat injuring itself in one, you can purchase a hi-tech training gimmick. I first encountered scat mats when at my wits end as to how to stop my cat from aggravating a neighbor by walking on the hood of his car leaving little kitty foot prints. The scat mat shocks the offending dog or cat when it jumps onto the mat. These devices are effective as long as they are in place. So my cat learned not to walk on the neighbors car for as long as he used the scat mat which wasn't very long. At least I had given my neighbor a viable solution, and he did not complain any more even though the cat continued to get on his car when he forgot to put the mat in place.

Bright dogs will learn to look for the scat mat and sometimes, but less often, the mouse traps. So make sure you use either for a minimum of two weeks to break the habit pattern. Dogs are basically obliging and want to please their leader but you must communicate your wishes in a way your dog can understand. With the canine genius, a scolding may be effective when he is caught on the furniture or has recently vacated it (are the cushions warm when you return home?). Grab Gigolo by the collar and drag him back the the scene of the crime. Tell him in no uncertain terms what an awful dog he is for climbing on the furniture while tracing a line from his eye to the warm cushion. Your scolding should not be so harsh that your dog is too frightened to make the connection between your upset and his misdeed. After Gigolo has gotten the message, make him hold a down-stay next to the piece of furniture for a few minutes. Be consistent and shortly your dog will comply!

GROOMING

Grooming your dog can be a pleasurable experience for her as well as you. Too often, however, it is wrought with anxiety. Poor Peaches, seeing the brush and nail clippers, and heads behind the couch thinking , "Oh no! They are going to pull my hair out and amputate my toes!'" And you hate it, because Peaches will not hold still and she is starting to snap at the brush, while your hand is holding it!

My dog gets a semi monthly make over consisting of a brushing out before and after a bath, nail clipping, teeth cleaning, ear cleaning, and the hair on his feet scissored or clippered. These procedures not only make him beautiful and pleasant to live with but they are essential for his good health! A complete make over can be accomplished in a half hour or less because he is cooperative and wants his special make over day cookie reward! In between his make overs, I brush Willy briefly several times a week. Australian Shepherds are hairballs.

All the angst normally associated with grooming and its possible progression to even worse problems can be prevented by just a few minutes of gentle work with your pup a couple times a week. Ideally you will get your pup at seven weeks of age (optimal for adjustment and bonding in a new home). As soon as your pups had a few days to acclimate to its new surroundings, begin rubbing her ears, all around her head, her legs and her feet (don't forget each and every little toe). Gently open her mouth and rub your finger around her gums, look in her ears and eyes, roll her over and pat her little puppy belly! Just mix this in with the usually petting of stroking the head and back. Your pup will get used to you touching all her body parts in a stress free way. Don't try to do everything in one sitting. If you are so inclined, learning to do basic TTouch on your pup will expedite this process.

Shortly, your pup will allow you access to all her two thousand and one body parts. Now start brushing her with a very soft brush and nipping *just the very tip* off her toe nails. ONLY brush for one to two minutes at a time and clip only a couple of nails each session. This is to get your pup used to these proceedings, *not* to do a full grooming in one sitting! Also gently clean an ear with a cotton swab. Continue to rug your finger around your pups gums. At the end of a grooming session, reward her with a little cookie.

Make sure your are not causing your pup any unnecessary discomfort. Do not use a metal toothed comb or brush on the bony parts of her face or legs. Do not pull her hair any more than absolutely necessary. Brush you dog regularly so she does not have mats that are uncomfortable to have removed. Proper grooming tools (consult your breeder or a professional dog groomer) will make the task easier on both you and your dog. This includes a tooth scaler. Being able to scale (scrap the tartar) from your dog's teeth will keep your dog's teeth and gums healthy without the risk of having to put her under anesthetic at the animal hospital!

Once you have started basic obedience training, you can place your pup on a sit, down, or stand stay when grooming. You will already be way ahead of the class because of your earlier work.

For those of you reforming an older pup or adult dog who dislikes grooming, solid obedience training is the key. To teach your dog to be polite for brushing, place him on a sit or down-stay *on leash.* Brush gently for just one to two minutes. Release your dog from the stay and reward him with a treat and lots of praise. This is one situation where I consistently use a food reward for good behavior. The next day, brush for just one minute longer. Gradually build up to the amount of time necessary to thoroughly groom your dog.

If your dog breaks the stay, use the appropriate correction. When you have built your sessions up to five minutes or more minutes, mix in some breaks. Release you dog from the stay for a minute of praise and petting. Then place him on another stay and resume brushing.

Ah, you say, "What about the ever traumatic dog bath?" I say, "It need not be." Peaches may not like her scrub in the tub but she can behave herself anyhow. Your dog's comfort and safety are paramount. If bathing outdoors with a hose, make sure the water is warm enough not to cause discomfort and that you do not blast your dog with a power setting on the nozzle. Set the nozzle on shower. If bathing your dog outdoors, you have the advantage of being able to tie your dog to prevent escape. ONLY TIE YOUR DOG WITH A QUICK RELEASE SLIP NOT. If you don't know how, ask a sailor (or consult a tie tying book). If your dog panics, you can release a slip knot before she hurts himself!

When bathing Rufus outside, put him on a stand-stay, if he knows one, or a sit-stay if not, and tie him with a quick release slip knot. Begin wetting him down at his *feet* and work up. Do not squirt him in the face! Do not get water in his ears. If he breaks the stay, stop and calmly correct the broken stay. Remember your goal here is not just to give your dog a bath but to teach him to behave for bathing for the rest of his life! After he is thoroughly wet, you can soap him, being very careful not to get soap in his eyes. Then rinse, starting with the highest point on his body, usually the head. If your dog is doing the abused hang dog pose (head down), gently lift his head with one hand while you rinse with the other. Then rinse down his neck, etc.

If your are bathing your dog inside, put a nonskid mat in the bottom of your bath tub. Carefully place him in the tub. Do not let him slip and fall. Unless you have access to a professional dog groomers tub, you will not have the advantage of tying your dog. Get someone to assist you in bathing your dog until he is well behaved. Have your assistant hold your dog by the collar while you bathe or vice versa. Proceed as outlined above.

You can prevent getting water shaken all over you by controlling you dog's head. Firmly hold your dog's muzzle in one hand. This will prevent shaking as it starts with the head and proceeds down the body. When you release your hold, quickly give a command to "Shake!" as your dog begins. This will teach the meaning of the word so you can have your dog shake his body on command and not until he his given the command. If your dog tries to shake before you have commanded him to do so, tighten your grip on his muzzle and tell him "no" (that is if you have properly taught him the meaning of "no."). Not only does Willy wait to shake after a bath until I have finished bathing him and closed the shower curtain so he will not get water all over the bathroom, but I can command him to shake outdoors after brushing to get the fly away hair off or dislodge snow before entering the house! Very handy.

Nail clipping is a particularly aggravating procedure to many dogs. I believe some dogs start off not liking to have their feet handled because they are ticklish. Then somebody (we all do it occasionally) quicks (cuts the nail too short into the blood vessel and nerve) the dog a couple of times. And Vois-la! You have a dog that is either panicky or aggressive when you try to cut his nails. Another possible ingredient in dogs becoming aggressive over nail clipping is the inadvertent crank of a dog's leg into an uncomfortable position, causing pain, especially in dogs with joint problems.

The preventive medicine, TTouch (see chapter on TTouch) is also part of the remodeling plan. Desensitize your dog to having his feet handled by starting TTouch away from the feet and gradually working your way down to being able to "touch" your dog's feet without contention. The next step, using TTouch to relax you dog, is to introduce the nail clipper by brushing it over the foot. Do not try to clip a nail until your dog accepts the clipper without a fuss. When you have achieved this step, you are ready to clip the first nail.

Place your dog on a sit-stay, clip the very tip of one nail. The point is not to properly trim the nail but to be able to clip it without causing you dog to panic or become aggressive. If your dog behaves, release him from the stay and make a big fuss including giving your dog his favorite dog cookie. Wait twenty-four hours. Then clip one more nail. Once you start, you must not stop until you have clipped one nail. You must not quit until you win but do quit as soon as you have won on just one nail.

You can use a procedure similar to those outlined above to teach your dog to acquiesce to ear cleaning and tooth scaling. It is best to have your veterinarian or a qualified professional dog groomer teach these procedures as well as how to express your dog's anal glands. However, I will briefly describe ear cleaning and tooth scaling for you here. Put your dog on a sit-stay and drop the leash to the floor. Now stand on the leash so your dog can't escape and both of your hands are free. If your dog breaks the stay at any point, stop immedi-

ately and correct the broken stay. Do not let either procedure deteri-
orate into a wrestling match...your dog may win. Keep control
through your good solid obedience training. Using a cotton swab
dipped in alcohol (unless directed otherwise by your veterinarian),
insert the swab into your dog's ear parallel to the side of your dog's
head. Since a dog's ear canal makes a sharp right angle turn inward
as long as you keep the swab parallel with the side of his head, you
will not injure your dog. Swab out the inside of your dog's ear thoroughly. If there is any usual looking discharge or odor, take your dog
to his veterinarian. After you have finished cleaning one ear, release
your dog from the stay for a short break and reward. Put him on
another stay to do the other ear. Do not use a swab in one ear and then
the other. Always start the second ear with a clean swab, so you do
not infect it with something that may be developing in the first ear
cleaned. Just like humans, dogs can have an infection in one ear and
not the other. Don't risk spreading an infection, even if the swab from
the first ear looks clean. If your dog is particularly opposed to ear
cleaning, you may have to start with baby steps, partially cleaning
one ear a day until you have fully cleaned both ears.

To clean you dog's teeth, begin just as you began ear cleaning.
Put your dog on a sit-stay and drop the leash to the floor. Now stand
on the leash so your dog can't escape and both of your hands are free.
Reach across the top of your dogs muzzle with one hand and squeeze
his lips in between the teeth of his upper and lower jaws forcing his
mouth open in a safe manner. Ninety-nine percent of all dogs will not
bite through their own lips! If yours will, get a new dog. Now starting at the gum line scrap the scaler down your dog's canine tooth
(big, long, sharp, pointy one) away from the gum. Repeat this stroke
until you have cleaned just that one tooth. Now release your dog from
his stay and praise and reward. Clean a tooth a day until your dog is
well behaved for the procedure. Then you can gradually build up to
doing all his teeth in one session.

Now I know some of you are going to write me and say, "Easier
said than done." Not really. Do you honestly have good solid obedience training in place? If so, you'll be surprised how easily you can
teach your dog a variety of things from that simple foundation. If you
do not have an adequate training base, do not try these procedures at
home. You will only make matters worse. If your dog's dislike of any

grooming procedures has deteriorated into aggression, please see the chapter on aggression toward humans and/or get a qualified professional trainer's help.

If you have taught your dog to politely accept grooming at home, she will receive better grooming if you take him to a professional. Please do not make fun of a newly clipped dog. It can embarrass them! I have had perplexed people call and ask why their Peaches hides behind the couch when returning home from the groomer? How insensitive. And how long would you like going to the hair dresser if your family made fun of you when you got a new do? Teaching your dog to accept thorough grooming also mean she will get better health care from your veterinarian. If your dog will hold still to have her ears, eyes, mouth and body examined, she will get a much more thorough examination. Both your veterinarian and your dog groomer will greatly appreciate your efforts.

HOUSETRAINING

Housetraining a dog to eliminate outside or paper training takes advantage of a dog's natural instinct to keep his "den" clean. As soon as a young pup starts eating solid food, the canine mother, under normal circumstances, begins the housetraining process. The mother begins the process by encouraging the pups to eliminate away from her and the den area. We humans artificially extend the "den" to include the whole house.

Housetraining requires both physical and mental self control. Most pups have sufficient physical self control to begin formal housetraining at ten to twelve weeks. Basic obedience training develops mental self control and therefore greatly enhances the housetraining process. With most pups, the process cannot be completed until they are about six to eight months old because pups do not develop sufficient self control until then. However, accidents do not have to occur in your home until the pup is six months old. Quite the contrary, if you implement the following program there will be very few mistakes and those that do occur are usually the result of human error.

Prior to beginning formal housetraining, a pup should be confined to a small room. Initially the floor (a hard surface) should be completely covered with newspaper. Soon the pup will choose one area in which to eliminate. When the spot has been chosen, begin gradually reducing the paper starting at the opposite end of the elimination area. Continue this process until there are just a few sections in the pup's chosen "bathroom". Once the bathroom area has been established, make sure the kitchen (food and water bowls) and bedroom (towel or throw rug) are separated from each other by three to four feet.

If your goal is housetraining (eliminating outside) you should begin taking the pup outside on a on a regular schedule even during this period of pre-housetraining "paper training". At ten to twelve weeks your pup will most likely begin to demonstrate some physical self control by "holding" itself over night or for longer periods during the day. When this begins, you are ready to begin formal house-training.

Housetraining requires the use of a dog crate. It will only be used for a short period of time. The crate should be large enough for your pup to stand, turn around, and lie comfortably, but no larger. Dogs do not dislike their crates. A dog's crate becomes its sanctuary, to which, the dog will retreat throughout its life, given access.

An alternative to caging your pup overnight is securing him/her on one to two feet of chain (indestructible) to your bed post over night. This method is preferable in most situations to caging because it aids in the bonding process. NEVER chain a pup when you will not be with it for safety reasons.

To housetrain your pup, confine it to the crate (or chain) overnight and to the crate (or outside) when you will not be home or cannot supervise your pup. A puppy needs to be taken outdoors first thing in the morning, shortly after meals, after periods of excitement (such as play time, arrivals, and departures), last thing at night, and about every two hours. Ask your pup, "Do you need to go out?" (or a similar phrase) and take the pup outside to the appropriate area.

Encouraging the pup to scratch at the door can lead to a destructive habit. To resolve the communication problem, hang a small bell on a short length of string on the frame of the door the pup exits to the bathroom. Every time you ask your pup "Do you need to go out?", take a front paw and ring the bell. Most dogs will catch on in one to two weeks, as long as you are consistent. This establishes an audible means of communication and thus ends those accidents by the door when nobody noticed Rover wanted to go out.

When walked for bathroom purposes, allow only five minutes. If more time is allowed, the pup may forget why he is outside. Besides, during inclement weather, more than five minutes is unpleasant and unnecessary. Praise the pup using the selected phrase

("GOOD boy to go out!") while the pup is eliminating.

If your pup completely eliminates (whatever you feel it needs to do at that time) reward the pup with supervised freedom in the house for one to two hours. Then confine it to the crate for ten minutes and take it outdoors again.

If the pup does not completely eliminate within its allotted five minutes, reconfine it to the crate for fifteen minutes and then take it outdoors again. Repeat this process until you are satisfied the pup has emptied itself. Then reward the pup with supervised freedom in the house. As the pup develops greater self control, decrease the frequency of bathroom walks thus increasing the amount of supervised freedom time.

For working families, housetraining will take twice as long as situations in which someone is usually home during the day. If at all possible, a family member should come home midday to walk the pup. If this is not possible, arrange to have a neighbor or someone else walk the pup at this time. Inconsistent lunch break walks will do more harm than good (dogs are animals of routine). A midday walk will not only accelerate housetraining, it is also in the best interest of the pup both mentally and physically.

With some larger breeds, even a lunch break will not allow sufficient exercise for proper physical development. In situations where caging the pup during the day would be unhealthy, a small room will be necessary for confinement. As described for pre-housetraining confinement, this room should have a "newspaper bathroom", "kitchen" and "bedroom" separated by at least three to four feet. Use a crate or chain at night to begin developing the capacity of the pup to hold himself. Under these circumstances, most pups will stop using the paper during the day when they are able to do so.

Ideally most dogs should spend a good portion of the day outdoors. Outdoor time improves or prevents coat and skin problems, decreases shedding, allows time for exercise and is less boring. Leaving the pup in a securely fenced yard or a dog kennel is an excellent solution to the working family dilemma. Never chain a dog for an extended period (longer than five minutes). Chaining can lead to barking, digging and aggression problems.

This method of housetraining will eliminate most destructive chewing because your pup will be supervised or confined throughout the teething stage. At approximately six to eight months of age, your pup will have his adult teeth, will have developed a high degree of mental self control through obedience training and will have physical self control. You will now begin the artificial expansion of the "den" to include the whole house by gradually weaning the pup out of the crate. BUT one step at a time, having the pup gradually earn the responsibility of the increased space. Initially, we increase freedom at night. Have your pup sleep loose in your bedroom only for two weeks. Then add the next smallest adjoining space and so forth in one to two week increments.

Next step is freedom when you are not present. Start with one half hour, and double time every one to two days. Confine your pup to one room only until he/she has been responsible in that space for the required amount of time(the length of your work day) for two weeks. Block off doorways with baby gates (one on top of the other if necessary) where there are no closable doors.

After the pup has kept this room clean for two weeks for the required amount of time, allow him access to this room plus the next smallest adjoining space. After one to two weeks of success at this level, add another room and continue with this process until the pup is responsible with complete freedom throughout the house. If at any point the pup backslides, drop back to the previous level for one to two weeks. You would not suddenly turn a child loose on its own, so do not dump too much responsibility on your young canine too quickly.

Should you catch your pup in the act of making a mistake or if a human error results in an accident found at a later time, you may scold the pup. (I personally do not scold after the fact as it is usually ineffective.) To do so, grab the pup by the collar or scruff and trace a line from the pup's eye to the accident several times as you verbally reprimand. DO NOT rub the pup's nose in the accident, causing it to be dirty (after all, you are teaching the dog to be clean)! Then quickly usher your pup outside to the appropriate "bathroom," using the selected phrase as you go. The pup need not remain outside for long—just enough time to make the connection. PLEASE keep in mind, if a correction is too frightening the pup will only focus on the punishment and will not make the connection between the scolding and wrongfully eliminating indoors.

Accidents should be cleaned with club soda (on carpeting) and white vinegar (on hard surfaces). These solutions will eliminate odors and staining if used immediately. Commercial cleaners often contain ammonia which is a component of urine. Ammonia draws the pup back to the same spot. Thoroughly re-clean soiled spots where commercial cleaners have been used. If you are attempting to housebreak an older dog who has indiscriminately soiled your carpeting, the carpeting <u>must</u> be steam or dry cleaned to eliminate the odors. Shaklee products, Basic G and Basic H are extremely successful in removing pet stains and odors.

By strictly following this program, housetraining will be a quick, painless process with few accidents for both you and your dog. This is a general outline of the housetraining process that covers most situations. Some circumstances may require other alternatives. If more detailed instruction is required or you are having problems, contact a qualified professional trainer.

HYPERACTIVITY

A truly hyperactive dog literally cannot sit still without chattering its teeth and salivating from the effort. Fortunately, these genetic disasters (usually created by back yard breeding) are rare. What is commonplace are normally highly active dogs, most often of the sporting and hunting breeds, mislabeled as hyperactive. Pet dog owners frequently select breeds based on appearance, popularity, availability (my neighbor's dog had pups), and/or their own misconception of such as the ever-popular Labrador and Golden Retrievers. These dogs, like most sporting and hunting breeds, were bred to run for hours. Mismanaged, their excess energy may be burned off chewing up the couch, racing through the house overturning furniture, bursting out the door, barking excessively, and leaping on everyone. In addition to sufficient exercise, active dogs must be on a low protein diet and must be well trained to control their exuberance and make enjoyable pets.

A typical complaint of owners of under-exercised dogs is that, "Flash races through the house every day at 4:00 PM,"…pick a time, but the dogs engaging in this behavior are fairly consistent in their schedules. No, just being outside in the yard will not sufficiently exercise your dog. It is a rare dog (just like it is a rare human) who will adequately exercise without some external motivation. No a game of fetch will not replace daily walking. Keep playing ball and letting Flash hang out in the yard but you must also walk your dog every day. A portion of your dog's daily walk needs to be aerobic. Medium to large dogs should get at least a one mile (approximately 15–20 minute) aerobic walk daily. Small dogs should get at least a half mile or 10-minute aerobic walk daily. By aerobic, I mean **no stopping.** Allow your dog an opportunity to eliminate before starting the aerobic portion of your walk. If most humans walk briskly, most dogs will have to trot. Not only does aerobic exercise vitalize your dog physically, but it causes the release of endorphins in the brain, producing a relaxed feeling of well being. Aerobic exercise also helps burn off that excess energy. A relaxed, tired dog is a well behaved dog! (Do not jog with a dog under two years of age. The growth plates in the long bones should be fused before being subjected to the pounding of jogging).

Feeding high protein dog food is like feeding your dog jet fuel when he only needs regular gasoline. High protein levels may contribute to "hyperactivity." For most dogs, the level of **protein should be 22% or less** (less for overweight or older dogs). Most popular dog foods are 26% or higher! High protein foods became a fad decades ago when high protein became popular for human diets. We have not yet caught on that excessive protein is not any better for our dogs than it is us. Also, there is some evidence that red dyes and artificial preservatives may contribute to hyper behavior and of course, sugar does. If your dog's food looks like fruit loops it is probably making him fruity too. Feed your dog a good quality dry dog food that contains meat as its primary source of protein, and that does NOT contain dyes, artificial preservatives, soybean, by products, or sugar.

Drugs are not an acceptable solution to hyper behavior in our pets any more than they are for our children! The silver bullet fix is temporary at best and cruel. How would you liked to be drugged so you would fit into an environment you did not choose? I refuse to train dogs medicated for their activity level. With their owners consent, I wean all medicated dogs off drugs before training, and I have successfully trained EVERY dog brought to me formerly drugged for behavioral problems! 100%! And their owners always state they are better behaved after training than they were on meds! If you are drugging your dog to make it fit your lifestyle, shame on you.

Good, solid obedience training in which your dog learns to respond on one command consistently in distracting situations will build the self control necessary for him to control his exuberance. If Flash can hold a thirty minute down stay in your veterinarian's waiting room, he has the self control to walk calmly through your house, not chew up the furniture or bark like a crazed maniac, to be courteous at the doors and in greeting people. In conclusion, resolving hyper behaviors requires a holistic approach of plenty of exercise, a healthy diet, and sound training, NOT DRUGS!

INTRODUCING YOUR NEW BABY TO YOUR DOG

A dog owner that plans to have children within the life span of his or her dog, needs to socialize the dog around babies and children of all ages from puppyhood. If you are planning on having children and are adopting an older dog, select one that has been raised around kids. Please do not wait until a week before the little bundle of joy is due to arrive, and call the local dog trainer for advice on how to introduce your new baby to your dog! I have answered this call many times. Even if you do not plan on having children, they are everywhere. And your dog needs to behave in their presence if for no other reason than legal liability.

The reason that children are the most frequent victims of dog bites is that kids trigger a dog's prey drive. In the wild, the pack does not prey on the twelve point buck at the head of the heard but on the young and feeble. These inferior animals are smaller, less coordinated, slower, sound and smell different than the rest of the herd. Unless your dog is well socialized around children, children may meet this description of prey. If your dog, from a young age, experiences the sights, sounds, and smells of children of all ages then he recognizes kids as a part of the normal repertoire for the human animal.

Besides the all important socialization of your dogs with children, there are several things you can do to ease the adjustment of a new baby into your dog's life. A week or so before the baby is due, brush up your dog's basic obedience training in a ten minute session very day. This will sharpen up your control of your dog and his self control. It is also special quality time between you and your dog. I know things get very busy once the baby is home, but you must continue to give your dog a little special attention each day. Keep up the training and do not forget to play a little fetch and take a daily walk with Buddy too. By doing these few small things, your dog will not feel abandoned and act out accordingly.

Bring home a receiving blanket with your new baby's scent and that of its mother and give it to your dog prior to the baby's arrival at home. This single small thing can help enormously. The humans will be excited and perhaps, nervous when the new baby arrives home. So will the dog. You can use your dog's recently polished obedience training to control his exuberance when the baby arrives. After you are settled in with the new baby, put your dog on a sit-stay **on leash** and show him the baby, having one person hold the baby and another handle the dog. Abundantly praise your dog's good behavior around the baby (he *is* holding a stay). Correct any inappropriate behavior. After this introduction, carefully supervise the dog when he is in the baby's presence. When the baby fusses, and your dog is too nosey about what is going on, put him on a down stay. Do not throw your dog outside. If you banish your dog from the house every time he tries to investigate the baby, your dog may become resentful of the baby. As long as your dog was successfully well socialized around babies and children from puppy hood, his adjustment to your new baby should go smoothly (maybe easier than your adjustment)! Most likely, your dog will love its new pack member even if it does smell funny and wake him up repeatedly in the middle of the night!

JUMPING

Mostly dogs jump to get and to give attention. This habit is almost as old as your puppy and began even before you got him. Pups are usually raised in some sort of pen. The first puppy to jump up on the side of the pen is the first one picked up. Later, when you got your pup home and cute little fellow jumped on your pant legs, you naturally bent over and pet him.

The standard jumping corrections (otherwise know as the three ancient tortures) kneeing the dog in the chest, smacking upside the head, and stepping on hind feet, sometimes will cause a decrease in the behavior, but rarely solve the problem. Worse, they often create a sneak jumper that jumps on your side or back to avoid the correction. You see, your dog still desperately wants your attention and is willing to withstand the corrections because jumping is the only way he knows how to ask.

To humanely and effectively end a jumping problem, we must give the dog a positive way to ask for attention. By teaching your dog to sit whenever he approaches you or you approach him, a light bulb will soon go on for him. He will have a positive means to ask for attention, and avoid any unpleasant correction, politely sitting facing you.

Since your dog knows sit from his basic obedience training (if he is not rock solid in this command, you will need to spend some time training), ending jumping is merely a matter of your <u>consistently</u> making your dog sit every time he approaches you or you approach him. <u>Consistency is the key</u>! One family member allowing the dog to jump occasionally can undermine the good efforts of all others involved. The real loser in this situation is your dog since mixed messages will result in the need for more correction—not to mention confusion. The so called "softy" in the family is actually being cruel to the dog.

Now let's look at some real life situations. You have just arrived on the scene and your dog is racing toward you in excitement. When he is a few feet from you, give a firm (not harsh) command to sit. This allows the dog time to slow down and wind up sitting at your feet. If the dog doesn't sit or he jumps, use the sit correction. If the dog sits, however briefly, praise the dog. Remember this is not a sit-stay, he need only sit. Should the dog make another attempt to jump, tell him to sit and apply the correction if necessary. As you can imagine, one excited greeting may involve several sits.

A slightly more difficult situation is getting through the door with the dog bouncing inside. Open the door slightly and give the command to sit. If the dog obeys, enter the house and praise warmly. If the dog does not obey, you have two options: 1) Open the door get hold of the dog and apply the sit correction, or 2) Shut the door, wait one minute and try again. It is the most effective in the beginning of training to apply a sit correction. After you have been working on this behavior for several weeks, then graduate to the second option. Once you have graduated to this option, do not open the door until your dog sits. The message being he will not get any attention until he is behaving.

Now let us look at introducing your dog to others. When company arrives at your home, or you and Buddy meet someone on the street, place your dog in a sit-stay at your left side (in the heel position). Ask the company or friend to approach the dog face to face. If your dog breaks the sit-stay, ask the approaching party to stop where he is or back up a step as you apply the sit-stay correction. Repeatedly go through the steps of having the party approach and back away as you correct your dog if he breaks the stay until your dog can be petted while holding the stay. In this way, your dog is getting a twofold correction; one—the jerk on the collar but more importantly, he will learn that he will not get any attention from the approaching party if he misbehaves.

Obviously, the first few times you attempt this, it will go much smoother if the procedure is explained to the approaching party in advance. As the dog progresses, it will not be necessary to have the party come up and then back away. Just place your dog in a sit-stay before someone approaches and then allow him to greet the dog. In situations involving a very young or shy child, it may be necessary to have another adult lead the child by the hand to introduce her to your dog.

Now that we have covered the major situations in which jumping occurs, let us look at the day to day minor ones. You have been around the dog for awhile and just want to give him a pat or a milk bone; have him sit first. You are watching TV and Buddy nudges you for some attention; have him sit before you pet him. Remember, the dog must be made to sit <u>every time</u> he approaches you or you approach him.

Shortly, usually within a few days, a wonderful thing will begin to happen. Your dog will occasionally come up and sit before you have a chance to tell him. Praise him! Praise him! Praise him! Tell the dog what a "good sit" he did. These little gifts must not be overlooked. You see, your dog is saying "Pet me, please?" And if his polite new manners are not acknowledged, he'll resort to his old demanding behavior of jumping.

The length of time varies with dogs, but eventually this sit in front should become automatic (without your giving the command). Usually, by the end of 2–3 weeks, you will find that your dog consistently sits before you have a chance to tell him. When you get to this point, stop using the verbal command all together. Apply the sit correction if the dog does not sit on his own anytime you approach him or he approaches you. Your success or lack thereof in ending the jumping problem will be directly proportional to your <u>consistency</u>!

If you want your dog not to jump 100% of the time, you must demand the sit-in-front—100% of the time.

Occasionally, one encounters a dog that is an extremely determined jumper or has malicious intent…means to knock you down to do you harm. Dogs with malicious intent have an underlying aggression problem and are best handled with the help of a professional trainer. The very determined jumper may require an additional correction of a jerk down on the training collar while he is in mid air followed by the sit correction.

I know the explanation of this simple method—having the dog

sit in greeting to replace the jump—is lengthy. However, it is easy and rewarding to put in effect. There is nothing so rude as a jumping dog or more pleasant than one that says, "Please pet me," with a polite sit in front.

LEASH BAULKING

Leash balking is refusing to walk on a leash. The dog may simply plant his feet and refuse to go forward or he may sit down, lay down, and in worst cases, throw tantrums when asked to walk on a leash. The most common cause of leash balking is improper leash training. The first mistake a dog owner generally makes is trying to leash train his pup on a short lead. A twenty-foot lead for small dogs and a thirty-foot lead for medium to large dogs prevents a lot of trauma usually associated with getting a pup or older dog accustomed to walking on a leash. The extra length of the lead also prevents your dog from negatively associating the restriction of the leash with you.

The new puppy owner can also prevent setting him or herself up as the bad guy by tying his pup to the bedpost at night on a short piece of chain when housetraining (see chapter on housetraining). This will kill two birds with one stone. Besides confining the pup for housetraining purposes, it allows the pup to fight out any resistance to the leash with an inanimate object and not his person. This technique alone often easily teaches a pup to yield to the leash when out walking. PLEASE NOTE, I am not advocating tying unless a responsible human is right there with the pup (very sound sleepers and children, do not qualify). If the pup twists up his collar during the night, the human should hear the pup's distress in time to prevent injury.

The worst mistake a new pup owner can make is giving in when his pup cries or throws a puppy tantrum when coaxed into following on the leash. This will very quickly teach the pup how to train it's owner! Throw a tantrum and daddy or mommy will stop walking and pick me up, is what the pup learns. By the time your pup is a little too heavy to carry, you will have a leash balking problem. Even the small breed dogs that are often carried out of convenience or for safety need to learn to walk properly on a leash for housetraining.

Leash balking can be prevented and usually, but not always, corrected by proper leash training through an exercise called "posting." Posting is done on a long leash called a longe line. For a small dog, a longe can be made out of twenty feet of clothesline and a lightweight snap hook. For larger dogs, it is best to purchase a thirty foot canvas lead from a pet shop. For very heavy or extremely strong dogs, a horse longe line without a chain leader may be used.

Posting consists of walking from Point A to Point B in complete **silence totally ignoring the dog.** Walk in a pattern of straight lines with the points thirty to sixty feet apart. Do pick a specific point to walk to, such as a tree or bush. Having a specific goal lends determination to your presentation to your dog. The pattern can be a square, rectangle, triangle, a five pointed star, etc. Vary your pattern and direction. At each point, stop for a slow count of ten to twenty. During your brief stop at each point, do not address your dog in any way. Do not even look at her! Look up at the clouds. This increases your dominant posture. Do not untangle your dog unless there is risk of injury or else a smart pup will soon learn to foul the leash to get you to stop walking. Post one to three times a day for five to ten minutes with at least a two-hour break in between sessions.

Once the balker learns that his tantrums are not controlling the handler and no-one is going to coax him, he will get up and walk. For older sulkier dogs, posting may need to include some rough terrain. Bumping across a few logs is not as pleasant as skating across a slick floor. This is not rocket science, just simple cause and effect. "If I (your dog) follow my person, it relieves the pressure on my neck." Not only will the dog be walking freely on the leash in a short amount of time but he will have learned the rudiments of paying attention. "If I want to know where my handler is going, when he is going to stop, and start, I must watch." AND, you have begun to establish yourself as pack leader! You are leading, your dog is following. All this from a five minute walk with your mouth shut!

If your efforts fail, meaning you did not completely ignore your puppy, hand the leash to a four year old child and go for a walk. After a brief period of coaxing the pup, the child will get bored and just drag the puppy where he (the child) wants to go. The trainer I apprenticed under used to give her little boy the job of leash breaking all the pups she bred, and this was the scenario that Joe and the puppies enacted.

To the uninitiated, posting may sound cold but most pups enjoy the freedom of the long leash and a pleasant walk out of doors. You can build a positive attitude toward training by confining a pup for fifteen minutes, dogs thirty minutes before each session. From the dog's point of view, posting is increasing his freedom and opportunities. Whereas, if your dog is playing in the yard or racing through the house, putting him on a leash, however long, is decreasing his freedom.

Occasionally I have encountered a dog so entrenched in leash balking that it required a professional trainer to resolve. This most often occurs in Airedales and giant breeds. With all dogs and especially with these breeds, it is best to never let leash balking develop by improper leash training or giving in to doggie theatrics.

LEG LIFTING: TERRITORIAL MARKING

Lifting a leg to urinate on an object is a dog's way of marking his territory. Although female dogs mark their territory also, they seldom engage in inappropriate leg lifting. The culprits here are the boys. Adolescent male dogs (approximately six months of age) may try marking your house when they have already been successfully housetrained. Older male dogs perfectly housetrained may begin to engage in this behavior when a female comes into season in your neighborhood. Since dogs can scent one part per ten million, he will be able to detect a female in a very large area! When introducing a male dog into a new environment such as a new home or when you take him visiting, he may also engage in this behavior. Another situation that may inspire your dog to mark, is having other dogs visit his territory. Sometimes marking is a defiant behavior of a dominant dog lacking a strong pack leader.

Neuter your dog as early as your veterinarian will perform the surgery to prevent this problem (four months at some hospitals)! If you have an older dog that lifts his leg, neuter him, too, unless he is of such an age or has other health problems that make surgery a serious life threat. Older dogs can be given an injection of female hormones that will act as a temporary castration. This has two advantages. The effects of the injection are almost immediate, within a few days. The effects of neutering take several months to be fully evident because the male hormones already circulating in your boy's system at the time of the surgery do not disappear over night. It takes a several months for circulating hormones to dissipate. Once neutered, however, only a very limited amount of testosterone can be produced. The second advantage of injecting older dogs with female hormones is that the injection will allow you to see what the benefits of neutering will be on your dog's behavior without subjecting him to surgery. However, many veterinarians do not offer this service. Some feel it may be detrimental to your dogs health. I do not believe it is as a one time thing. Used repeatedly, it may cause some side effects, but I am not suggesting injecting your dog more than once. The other drawback is that the female hormones can be expensive, depending on your dog's weight.

Many owners, especially men, argue that they do not wish to neuter their dogs for a variety of reasons. Often the guys think it is cruel to neuter their four-legged male counterparts for psychological reasons. Get over it! If you want the best behaved pet, neuter. Not only is it necessary to prevent and to resolve leg lifting, neutering makes a dog more tractable and less likely to engage in other unacceptable behaviors like running away from home. Not to mention, preventing adding to the millions of unwanted dogs put to death every year in this country.

The second most common reason owners do not wish to neuter their dogs is the desire to breed. If your primary reason for having a dog is a pet, DO NOT breed your dog. Breeding even the best behaved male may result in leg lifting problems! Stud dogs are often so filthy that they can never be allowed indoors. Sometimes, even neutering will not help with leg lifting after a dog has been bred. Why risk ruining your dog as a pet? If you want one just like your boy, go back to his breeder and buy another pup. You are more likely to get one just like the good old boy you have from his parents than you are if you breed him anyhow! But you say, he is so beautiful, smart, sweet…is he truly an outstanding representative of his breed? Have your dog evaluated by several professional handlers and breeders including temperament testing. Even if he is judged to be of superior breeding quality, you will still be risking his acceptability as a pet if you breed him!

Next step in preventing or reforming a leg lifter is obedience training. If Butch is not already trained, do so immediately. If he is, brush up his training in a daily ten-minute session until the problem is resolved. This training not only is the foundation for building the self control Butch needs to refrain from marking but it clearly establishes you as pack leader. While reforming Butch, do not allow him unsupervised access to your home. When Butch is home alone, he should be caged or outside in a safe fenced outside yard or kennel. He should also be thus confined when you are home but cannot keep an eye on him. If he was truly well behaved prior to the beginning of the marking episode and you jumped on the problem as soon as it started, it will only take a short time to resolve it.

OK, Butch is neutered, solidly obedience trained, therefore, respects you as pack leader, and has been completely housetrained AND, he has started marking in your house. What to do? First, have him examined by your veterinarian to make sure he is not ill. Animals have an uncanny ability to communicate their needs. Butch may be marking or urinating right in front of you as his way of asking for help. I particularly suspect a health problem when a dog has been well behaved prior to the onset of marking and there have been no apparent reasons for the precipitation of the behavior such as having a dog visit in your home.

If your veterinarian gives Butch a clean bill of health, a good old fashioned scolding is the answer. You <u>must</u> catch Butch in the act. If necessary to nab him, have Butch trail a leash or six feet of clothesline. Holding him firmly by the collar, put his face right up to the spot he marked and trace a line with your finger from his eye to the soiled spot telling him all the while what a bad dog he is. Growl at him…make your voice low and guttural. Duration is the key. Scold for one minute by your watch as you repeatedly trace a line back and forth from Butch's eye to the soiled spot. Then put him on a down stay at the scene of the crime for one to three minutes. After the stay, march him to the door and send him outside to further contemplate his sin. Do this every time Butch attempts to lift his leg.

Following up the scolding with the down-stay is important for two reasons. Dogs get embarrassed just as humans do. If you have ever gotten a speeding ticket you know that it is humiliating to sit on the side of the road with those red and blue lights flashing even if you are out of state where no one knows you (not that this has ever happened to me!). The second reason for the down-stay is that the down is a submissive position in dog psychology as you know from having read the chapter on pack behavior. When you, the pack leader, put your dog down, you are saying, "I am the boss and I will not tolerate this behavior!"

When taking your male (or female) dog visiting, always potty walk him or her after arriving at the home in which your dog will be a guest (yes, even if h or she went before leaving home). Make sure your dog is on empty. Although males usually hold back a little urine for marking, should **you** make a mistake handling Butch there will be less damage if he has limited ammo. Take Butch into your host's house on leash. Put him on a down stay near you until he is calm (ten minutes or so). If he has had no prior history of leg lifting, and, of course, it is OK with your hostess, you may then release him from the stay but let him trail his leash as a reminder to behave and so you can quickly get a hold of him. **Watch him closely.** This is particularly important if there are other dogs in the house. If Butch is well behaved at home but has had a history of leg lifting elsewhere, do not release him from the stay accept to take him outside. After several visits to this one particular home without misbehavior, then you may try releasing him briefly from the stay. **Watch him closely.** If Butch is currently lifting his leg in your home, DO NOT take him visiting! How rude to take an ill behaved dog into another's home even if it is family!

Although usually not considered as serious as marking in your home, marking outdoors can also be a problem. If Butch is urinating on your flowers and shrubs, use moth flakes to repel him from the area. Naphthalene is the best dog repellent. It is the active ingredient in may commercially produced dog repellents (which are way over-priced). **Naphthalene is poisonous!** So do not use moth balls. Your dog may wolf down a couple of those white marbles before he gets a snout full of the offensive odor of naphthalene. Three to four moth balls could cause illness. However, moth flakes can be mixed in dirt or mulch on flower beds or around a shrubs giving your dog a good whiff of the repulsive odor and preventing him from going any far-ther.

If moth flakes are impractical in your situation, either because it frequently rains, which washes them away, or because you fear the use of poison around small children, then an electrified shock wire enclosing the gardens and shrubs will completely cure Butch. A low voltage fence charger designed to keep dogs and rabbits out of home gardens will not harm children, although touching a hot wire may frighten them. The trainer I apprenticed under had a passion for growing roses and a very dominant male dog that thought the rose bushes were ideal marking posts. He only lifted his leg once on the bushes inside the newly installed electric fence wire. The current traveled right up his stream, and he never peed on another rose bush for the rest of his life! That's what you call a shocking experience!

LICKING

Licking is one of the ways a dog expresses affection. Part of the joy of having a canine companion is an occasional "kiss." However, excessive licking can become quite annoying. Sometimes it is simply an excessively oral dog (often retrieving breeds or mixes), and sometimes it is to get salt or yummy lotion from your skin.

Excessive licking can be easily prevented in puppies. If your pup licks when you reach to pet him, SMOOTHLY remove your hands. Do not jerk your hands away because fast movements may excite your pup to leap up for another try. Replace your hands on the pup immediately. Repeat this procedure three to four times so your pup has an opportunity to make the connection between licking and the removal of the objects of affection, your hands. If your are dealing with a very young, untrained pup, turn your back on him and walk away if he persists in licking after three to four attempts to pet him.

If your pup follows you leaping up and licking, squirt him in the mouth with a mixture of 1/4 white vinegar and 3/4 vinegar. Do not use a spray bottle that once contained a cleaner. Any residue may be harmful to your pup's eyes should you miss his mouth. For the same reason, use only white vinegar. Cider vinegar has sediment in it that may lodge in your pup's eyes causing irritation. Have your pup trail six feet of clothesline that has been soaked in Grannick's Bitter Apple (the most effective doggie no chew product). Step on the trailing line just before squirting your pup to prevent his escape from correction. Otherwise, he may quickly devise a lick and run game. This correction is only to be used on a persistently bold pup and it should not be used excessively. A pup of this temperament needs to begin obedience training as soon as possible.

When you are working with a trained pup, after three to four attempts at petting and removing your hands when he licks fail, put the pup on a stay leash length (six foot) away from you for one minute. This is puppy time out. Do not have the pup hold the stay longer or he may forget what got him stuck on the stay. The time out shows the pup that the objects of affection, your hands, will be out of reach when he licks. The stay also forces the pup to use self control, thus requiring him to calm <u>himself</u> down and it places you back in control, a leader position. Dogs of any age are less likely to engage in behaviors that annoy their leaders.

Grannick's Bitter Apple can be used in conjunction with the above procedures. Bitter Apple is an extract of sour green apples in an alcohol base originally developed by a veterinarian to stop dogs from chewing on their sutures and coats. It is antiseptic and will not harm your skin. Most ordinary fabrics are color fast to Bitter Apple. Spray Bitter Apple on your hands and legs, if necessary, every few hours. If you do not taste good, your pup will not want to lick you as much.

Besides expediting the above procedures when sprayed on the hands of adults, Bitter Apple is also a quick and easy fix for children that are being molested by a puppy. Spray Bitter Apple on the hands, legs, pant legs, or shirt sleeves as necessary. (Not only will the Bitter Apple discourage the puppy but it may have the added bonus of stopping thumb sucking and finger nail biting by your child). Of course, it is essential that you instruct children in acceptable ways to pet and play with a dog. Always supervise children and pets!

MOUNTING BEHAVIOR

I saw a cartoon once with a little canine Romeo attached to a woman's leg. In the next frame she had strapped sand paper to her leg. I do not know if this solution will cure the Romeo in your house, but it was good for a chuckle. Mounting behavior is a nasty habit almost always confined to the male of the canine species. It is especially prevalent among small dogs. I am not sure why this is so unless the horny little devils are just thwarted by the females of their own species and decide to latch onto whatever else is available, usually the leg of an adult or any available part of a child.

Mounting is normal young puppy play behavior. As long as it is with a pup's litter mates, ignore it. If a young pup mounts any part of a human, discourage the behavior immediately. It is also a good idea to discourage mounting the family cat. If it is a very young pup just a gentle scruff shake and a firm "no" should suffice . A scruff shake is performed by grasping your pup by the scruff (loose skin on the back of the neck), elevating his front feet off the floor a couple of inches, and gently but firmly shaking him from side to side once or twice. **Not too violently!!!** If you scare the wits out of your pup, he will have none to make the connection between his amorous advances and the negative consequence. Scruff shakes should only be used in young puppies (under four months of age) and sparingly so. If over used you may either teach your pup to be frightened of you or teach him to ignore you, depending on the severity of the shakes.

Like all other problem behaviors, an ounce of prevention is worth a pound of cure. Neuter your dog as early as your veterinarian will perform the surgery to prevent this problem (four months at some hospitals)! If you have an older dog that mounts, neuter him, too, unless he is of such an age or has other health problems that make surgery a serious life threat. Older dogs can be given an injection of female hormones that will act as a temporary castration. This has two advantages. The effects of the injection are almost immediate, within a few days. The effects of neutering take several months to be fully evident because the male hormones already circulating in your boy's system at the time of the surgery do not disappear over night. It takes a several months for circulating hormones to dissipate. Once neutered, however, only a very limited amount of testosterone can be produced. The second advantage of injecting older dogs with female hormones is that the injection will allow you to see what the benefits of neutering will be on your dog's behavior without subjecting him to surgery. However, many veterinarians do not offer this service. Some feel it may be detrimental to your dogs health. I do not believe it is as a one time thing. Used repeatedly, it may cause some side effects, but I am not suggesting injecting your dog more than once. The other drawback is that the female hormones can be expensive, depending on your dog's weight.

Many owners, especially men, argue that they do not wish to neuter their dogs for a variety of reasons. Often the guys think it is cruel to neuter their four-legged male counterparts for psychological reasons. Get over it! If you want the best behaved pet, neuter. Not only is it necessary to prevent and to resolve mounting, neutering makes a dog more tractable and less likely to engage in other unacceptable behaviors like running away from home. Not to mention, preventing adding to the millions of unwanted dogs put to death every year in this country.

The second most common reason owners do not wish to neuter their dogs is the desire to breed. If your primary reason for having a dog is a pet, DO NOT breed your dog. Breeding even the best behaved male may result in mounting and leg lifting problems! Stud dogs are often so filthy that they can never be allowed indoors. Sometimes, even neutering will not help with leg lifting after a dog has been bred. Why risk ruining your dog as a pet? If you want one just like your boy, go back to his breeder and buy another pup. You are more likely to get one just like the good old boy you have from his parents than you are if you breed him anyhow! But you say, he is so beautiful, smart, sweet...is he truly an outstanding representative of his breed? Have your dog evaluated by several professional handlers and breeders including temperament testing. Even if he is judged to be of superior breeding quality, you will still be risking his accept-ability as a pet if you breed him!

Next step in reforming Romeo is basic obedience training. If he is not already trained, do so immediately. If he is, brush up his train-ing in a ten-minute session every day until the problem is resolved. This training not only is the foundation for building the self control Romeo needs to refrain from mounting, it also clearly establishes you as pack leader. One does #$@&* the pack leader.

Every time Romeo mounts anyone, immediately remove him from his victim, scold him telling him what an awful, nasty boy he is in a low guttural tone and put him on a one to three minute down-stay. Shorter stay for pups, longer stay for older dogs. Then release him from the stay. If he gets fresh again, repeat the procedure. The more often he tries, the more often you have an opportunity to teach him this is an unacceptable behavior! If you nip this problem in the bud, it is usually easy to stop. If the behavior is well established, you will have to be consistent and persistent.

MOUTHING (playful chewing on hands)

Mouthing is playful chewing on your hands and arms. It is normal in young pups. Since pups do not have hands with which to explore their environment, they use their mouths. They also use their mouths to play and get attention from litter mates and other dogs. Mouthing also can be a display of affection. I knew a grand old dog that would greet guests at the garden gate. She would escort them to the house by ever-so-gently placing her mouth over their arm and leading them to the door. Mouthing is more prevalent in dogs bred to use their mouths in their work such as retrievers and some herding breeds.

Unfortunately, mouthing often becomes excessive and uncomfortable to the pup's object of affection. When a pup is weaned from his mother and litter mates prior to the sixth week of age, he is deprived of the opportunity to learn an acceptable level of mouthing both in strength and duration. It is during the sixth to the seventh week of growth that the pup is taught by his mother how hard and how often a leader will tolerate mouthing. Brothers and sisters teach on another what is excessive on a sibling level. These lessons are naturally much easier learned by a canine from a canine. Bottle raised puppies are often excessive mouthers and have other behavioral problems due to their lack of canine contact.

Too often excessive mouthing is <u>taught</u> by humans through inappropriate play. Rough-up-around the face games are very popular with puppy owners. If you teach the pup that roughhousing with his mouth is a desirable way to play with humans, it is unfair to be upset when he tries to initiate a game by mouthing when you are not in the mood. Tug-o-war is the worst game you can play with a dog. It teaches the dog to use its mouth aggressively against you. In a game of tug-o-war, your pup learns to bite down hard (often growling) and vie for control against you. This lowers you from leader to a sibling or equal level. These are seriously undesirable lessons which can lead to aggression problems besides causing excessive uncomfortable mouthing.

Another way humans inadvertently teach mouthing is through poor methods of correction. Lecturing as you shake your finger in your pup's face is not only ineffective, but it's like dangling a wiggling worm in front of a fish. Smacking in the face creates a whole slew of problems. Violence often incenses violence. If your pup is of dominant temperament, he may fight back by nipping. Even with less aggressive temperaments, many pups will learn to respond physically to such punishment out of frustration or self defense. Holding the mouth shut to correct mouthing frequently frustrates pups to the point that they try even harder to use their mouth.

So what do you do about this annoying and sometimes quite uncomfortable problem? First, you must stop playing any games that feed into mouthing, and stop using poor methods of correction. Obedience training alone often ends a mouthing problem because if promotes you to a dominant position. One does not chew on the pack leader. Proper training gives you the control and the dog the self-control to straighten out even the most persistent mouthers.

If your dog mouths when you reach to pet it, SMOOTHLY remove your hands. Do not jerk your hands away as fast motion will excite a pup causing him to leap up for another nip. Replace your hands on the pup immediately. Repeat this procedure three to four times so the pup has a chance to make the connection between his mouthing and the removal of the objects of affection, your hands. If you are dealing with a very young, untrained pup, turn your back, and walk away if the pup persists after three to four attempts to pet him.

If this pup follows you leaping up and nipping as you go, squirt it in the mount with a mixture of 1/4 white vinegar and 3/4 water. Make sure your squirt bottle or gun has never contained a cleaner. The residue of a cleaner could injure your dog's eyes if a squirt misses the mouth, but under normal circumstances, this solution of vinegar will not injure the eyes. This correction is only to be used on persistent aggressive pups and it should not be used excessively. A pup of this nature needs to begin obedience training immediately.

When you are working with a trained pup, after three to four attempts of petting, and removing the hand when the pup mouths, put the pup on a short stay away from you for one minute (six feet away is sufficient). This shows the pup that the objects of affection, your hands, will really be out of reach when he uses his mouth. The sit stay also forces the dog to use self-control, thus calming himself, and places you back in control, a leader position.

Grannick's Bitter Apple can be used in conjunction with the above procedures. It is also a quick and easy fix for children. Spray Bitter Apple on the hands and pant legs of children every few hours. Bitter Apple is an extract of very sour apples in an alcohol base originally developed by a veterinarian to stop dogs from chewing out surgical sutures or their hair coats. Therefore, it is completely antiseptic and will not injure children. However, not only will their hands and clothing taste bad to your pup, but to themselves also. This could have the added bonus of stopping thumb sucking and finger nail biting. Of course, instruct and supervise the children in acceptable ways to pet and play with a dog.

Mouthing can be quite annoying minor problem and occasionally, a severe problem where small children or the thin skinned elderly are the victims. However, it is easily prevented and usually easily corrected.

PREDATORY BEHAVIORS (chicken killin' and the like)

Whenever I am asked about chicken killin' dogs the story of Beaureguard comes to mind. Years ago I had a very kind city couple bring a Beagle mix named Beaureguard in for training. They rescued him from the hills of North Carolina while on vacation. This couple was taking a scenic drive when they happened upon two men armed with shotguns chasing a little dog down the road. The city couple opened the car door and the pup hopped right in. Guess he figured, any port in a storm! The men chasing the dog told the couple that he had been raiding their chicken coop stealing eggs and killing the birds. They were going to put an end to his miserable little life if they ever saw him again. So the couple spirited the pup away to their New York home where, the newly named Beaureguard, took up tap dancing on the top of their grand piano among other uncouth behaviors. What is it they say? "No good deed goes unpunished." The happy ending to the story is that Beau was reformed through training to become a well behaved, much loved little rascal.

Chicken killing, and similar behaviors used to be a more common problem than it is in today's urban world. Although if it is a problem in your area, it is a life and death one since livestock owners are perfectly justified in shooting the offending dog. As a kid growing up in farming country, I heard of many tortures devised to punish the egg stealin', chicken killin' , coop raidin,' varmint of a dog. Many of these "corrections" were cruel and all were ineffective.

First of all, your dog should not be running at large. Most all of us live close to dangerous roads. If you and your dog are blessed to live in an area remote enough for him to run loose, it is still only acceptable if he stays home and out of trouble. If he does not, keep him in the house with you or pen him up when he is to be outside unattended! NEVER CHAIN A DOG.

Now if Beaureguard is after your own chickens, here is a 100% cure. Select a cull chicken or rooster from your flock. That nasty rooster that pecks your legs when your back is turned will do nicely! Your chicken will not be harmed if you set this up correctly, but it may throw a hen off egg laying temporarily. Unbeknownst to Beau (do not let him watch you set up), place a sheet of cardboard on the ground near the chicken pen. Drive a stake through the center of the cardboard. Run a shock wire from a **4 volt or smaller** fence charger designed for use on dogs and small animals up through the cardboard at the stake . Now tie the chicken by a leg to the stake and attach the wire to the another leg. Throw some scratch on the cardboard. Turn on the fence charger. The cardboard insulates the chicken from the ground. It should be large enough that the chicken can't get off it but not so large that your dog will be able to get all fours on it at once thus insulating himself. The most reaction I have ever seen on the part of the chicken, is a cluck when the charge comes on and then they contentedly peck away at the feed. Now go touch the chicken. That's right, I said go touch the chicken! You do want to make sure it is giving off a shock before you endanger its life, and if you have used a small fence charger the shock will not injure you. It will startle you even though you know it is coming!

Now you are ready to let Beau casually find the "escapee" chicken. Just walk out in the vicinity of the set up with Beau. Don't drag him up to the chicken. We want all set ups to appear as natural as possible. Do not say a word when your dog goes for the chicken and gets zapped. No laughing either. To the uninitiated, laughing at a dog getting a mild shock may sound morbid but you would have had to experience the needless killing of your own helpless penned chickens to understand. We want Beau to think that the chicken has acquired electrifying powers so he will leave them be even when you are not present. If you yell at him as he attacks he will associate the correction with you and not the bird.

Set Beau up for several days in a row. You may need to use a different chicken and move them to different locations if your dog is a die hard chicken killer. If chicken killing is a relatively new behavior, one experience is usually enough, BUT set Beau up for at least a few days spread over a two-week period to be sure.

One more story. My business partner once owned a beautiful huge male Akita that was dumb as a door nail and aptly named Demon. I had a pet baby goose at the training center that managed to get inside the security run at the same time that big lug escaped his kennel. Demon attacked my goose, but I got to the scene in time to stop him from killing it. The goose was seriously injured, including a punctured lung. I put the goose in a clothes basket in the kitchen near the wood stove to keep it warm. The house dog, also a large male Akita, but quite gentle, had also previously been attacked by Demon. The house dog adopted that little goose like they were kindred victims suffering from the same ill fate. He would lie by the basket watching over the bird and even licked him to help smooth his wounds. The goose endured a long recovery but it did live. The house dog never abandoned his post beside the basket until the goose was released to live outdoors!

And the rest of the story is, I set Demon up with an electrified chicken (didn't have another goose). He shocked himself once and then you couldn't drag him near poultry for the rest of his dumb life. It is a highly effective correction.

Now I would not suggest trying to tie a bunny or other small furry creature up by the leg and wiring it. If your dog is harassing your bunny or other caged critter, try working right about turns using the critter as a distraction until your dog will no longer take his eyes from you to look at the caged animal. Then work stays near the cage to build even more self control in your dog. If you catch your dog harassing the animal, scold him tracing a line from his eye to the cage and make him hold a down stay at the scene of the crime for several minutes. If after a couple of weeks of right about-turns, stays and scoldings, your dog is still at it, shock wire off the area. You can run a shock wire a foot off the ground on PVC pipe around the perimeter of the critter's cage to stop the harassment. Put the wire far enough back from the cage that your dog's approach is thwarted before the caged animal is terrorized. Leave the wire turned on for at least two weeks. Then you may turn it off but leave the wire in place for another couple of weeks. Turn it back on if your dog regresses. After a few weeks of no terrorist attacks by your dog, you may try removing the wire. If your dog reverts to his old bad ways, put the wire back up and leave it.

SCRATCHING & JUMPING ON DOORS AND WINDOWS

Of all the things dogs tend to scratch on besides themselves, doors and windows are the most common. Sometimes an owner encourages scratching on the door during housetraining only to find later what a destructive and annoying habit it can become. Sometimes dogs just pick it up on their own. Dogs scratch and jump on doors when they want outside and when they want inside. They scratch and jump on doors and windows when they see something outdoors they want to get to such as a mail person, meter reader, passer-by, another dog, a cat or a squirrel.

Scratching on doors is usually very easily corrected by simply teaching your dog courtesy at the door (see the chapter by that name), because the exercise teaches respect for the door way. If you have thoroughly taught and enforced courtesy at the door and your dog is still scratching the door, get some cheap, kiddies birthday balloons and blow them up tight. Tape the easily burst balloons to the area of the door your dog is scratching. Once the door starts blowing up on her, she'll most likely quit scratching and jumping on it. I only know one dog that likes to pop balloons and my sister owns it, so you are most likely safe from that foil.

If you own a really persistent door jumper/scratcher who ignores the balloons or regresses when they are no longer taped to the door or if you are afraid your dog will swallow a popped balloon (I do not consider this a threat, but a client brought it up a couple of years ago), there is another correction. This correction is near fool proof but requires a little more effort on your part. You can attach a shock wire charged by a **4 volt *only*** fence charger to your door. These fence chargers are designed to keep dogs and rabbits out of vegetable gardens and will scare, but will not injure your dog. The shock wire is best installed on insulators such as those used for electric fencing. If you do not wish to put holes in your door, the wire can be duct taped on, but it is much more difficult to install with tape so that it does not ground out, than it is with insulators. Do not let your dog watch you install the wire. Once installed, plug in the charger and let Knucklehead have at the door. Remember you want her to think that the correction comes from the door and not from you so, do not say a word. If your dog associates the correction with you and not the door, she may continue to jump and scratch when you are not present. This is the beauty of a set up. Set ups work without your being present and, therefore, teach your dog not to <u>ever</u> engage in the unwanted behavior instead teaching her not to do it just when you are home. Leave the wire turned on for two weeks; then turn it off but leave it attached to the door for two more weeks. Turn it back on for at least two more weeks if your dog jumps up or scratches even once. After the wire has been turned off for two weeks and there has been no misbehavior, you can take it off the door. Throughout the period of using the shock wire, make sure you are insisting on courtesy at the door also.

Correcting jumping and scratching at windows is similar to correcting it at doors. Every time your dog engages in the unwanted behavior, put her on a down-stay in front of the window for a minute or two. The down is a submissive posture and when you, the pack leader, put your dog down, you are saying, "I am the boss and I will not tolerate that behavior!" If your dog is so excited by something she sees outside you may have to snap on her leash and work right about-turns to get her attention focused on you before you can successfully get her to hold a stay. Balloons can also be taped to windows just like doors. If you have a small dog that is jumping up on a couch or chair to look out the window and then jumps or scratches on it, try removing the piece of furniture so it is not possible. If you have a larger dog and NO small children or cats in your home, you can employ another set up for window sills. Get several mouse traps (the little ones, NOT rat traps). Set them and place the traps on the window sill, one trap every foot or so. Cover each trap with a tissue sprayed with Grannick's Bitter Apple. The tissue is to disguise the mouse trap. The Bitter Apple is to make the tissue offensive tasting should your rascally dog decide to snatch it. Now when your dog puts her paws on the window sill, it will snap at her! Once the window sill starts to fight back, most dogs will stop jumping and scratching on them. Set your dog up every day for at least two weeks (a critical learning period in dogs). Remember do not let your dog see up set her up!

Although I am not a big fan of training gimmicks, I like to experiment with new products in hopes of finding something really useful. Of course, I do this on my own a animals before recommending a product to a client. At my wits end as to how to stop my cat from aggravating a neighbor by walking on the hood of his car leaving little kitty foot prints, I purchased a scat mat . The scat mat shocks the offending dog or cat when it jumps onto the mat. These devices are effective as long as they are in place. So my cat learned not to walk on the neighbors car for as long as he used the scat mat which wasn't very long. At least I had given my neighbor a viable solution and he did not complain any more even though the cat continued to get on his car when he forgot to put the mat in place. The scat mat can be attached to the area of the door on which your dog jumps or scratches and may be very effective on a light colored door since the white mat will blend in with it.

There is also a new invention on the market called a zone collar. The zone collar emits a mild shock when your dog comes with in a preset range of a transmitter, saucer sized disc. The zone collar will stop door and window jumping and scratching for as long as the dog wears the collar. However, unless you have a really dumb dog, once you remove the collar, your dog will regress to the old unwanted behavior because he associates the correction with the collar and not the door. This is what I call collar-dependent behavior. The other problem with the zone collar is that since the dog must wear it all the time and the electrical contact points may rub sores on your dog's neck.

Let me repeat that properly training courtesy at the door is successful in stopping door jumping and scratching 90% of the time as long as you train consistently and for a the recommended amount of time. Down-stays and mouse traps almost always cure window jumping and scratching. The more gimmicks you use, the more likely you will create undesirable side effects in your dog such as being afraid to go through the doorway, but more importantly, you don't want your dog's good behavior to be dependent on external stimuli and not internal self control.

SELF-GROOMING

Self-grooming, or, your dog's washing himself is a fault in relatively rare situations. If your pup self-grooms to excess or compulsively, it can result in an unhealthy condition of the skin or dramatic hair loss. Consult your veterinarian. Occasionally, a dog will perform a self-grooming ritual at night, keeping his owners awake. Although for bonding and protection, it is best to have your dog sleep in your bedroom, the most obvious solution to this situation is to have your dog sleep in another room. There are a few other things you can try. Thoroughly brush your dog several times a week and bathe your dog once or twice a month. If your dog is well groomed by you, he will have less to do himself. You may also use Grannick's Bitter Apple shampoo. It will make your dog hair taste nasty, and your dog will be less likely to self-groom. However some self-grooming is healthy. Lastly, put your dog on leash at bedtime and on a down-stay near the bed. When your dog starts grooming himself, give the leash a little jerk and tell your dog "No!" Do this repeatedly until your dog gives up on grooming or you fall asleep.

SEPARATION ANXIETY

Separation anxiety is a term dog folks have borrowed from human psychology, but it does aptly describe the distress suffered by some dogs when left home unattended. These dogs panic when alone, resulting in problem behaviors—including excessive salivation, urination and defecation, destructive chewing, racing through the house knocking things over, and scratching at doors and windows to escape. The range of behavior can be from mild bouts of destructive chewing to a major trashing of the house. Unless relieved the anxiety and resulting behaviors usually worsen over time.

Separation anxiety is most commonly the result of a dog's having changed homes. The trauma of changing homes, especially more than once, often causes insecurity resulting panic that it will happen again. A radical change in an owner's schedule may trigger the behavior. Someone who was home in a pup's formative months, but then out of the home the home such as the school teacher who gets a pup at the beginning of summer break and then returns to work in the autumn, or a stay-at-home mom or dad who returns to the work force. Separation anxiety can develop when a pup is raised by an over protective, clingy owner. I have encountered separation anxiety when a family is using a pet sitter rather than a boarding kennel.

Like nearly every problem, separation anxiety is more easily prevented than cured. If you are raising a pup, leave it home alone at least once a week. This will teach the pup that there is no need for panic because you will return. When departing, crate your pup WITHOUT a big parting lecture or goodbye. A big goodbye builds up emotion. Then you depart and the puppy feels miserably let down.

Prepare knuckle bones according to the recipe in the chapter on chewing or purchase "natural bones" from a pet store and stuffed them with doggie beef jerky to make a special treat to occupy your dog while your are gone. When you are ready to leave just toss the special chew toy and your pup in his crate and leave (after a potty walk, of course). When you return, NO big hello. Dogs obviously have very good memories, and if you whoop them up when you return, in hindsight, the time you were gone will seem bleak. Now, remove the special treat from your dogs crate. He is only to get them when he will be left alone. This prevents the novelty from wearing off, and thus the effectiveness of the "puppy pacifier." Some dogs learn to look so forward to getting their special bone that they run and get in their crate when they see you prepare to depart!

Pet sitters work fine with some dogs but not with others. If you wish to use a sitter, she must be someone the dog knows well prior to your leaving your dog in her care. It is best not to use a pet sitter with a young or high-strung dogs, as they are less resilient to disruption of their routine. The protective dog may be conflicted by having to allow someone into his home when his family is not present. Young, high-strung, and protective dogs should be boarded at a kennel. It is less disruptive for them to be out of their environment completely than to have their routine in their homes altered by the absence of their family, and the invasion of a relative stranger. It is advisable to board any dog at least once in its first year when it is most flexible to new experiences. Even if you do not plan to board your dog in the future, should an emergency call you out of town, boarding your older dog will go much easier on him with the memory of past experience in a kennel and your having returned. Of course, it should go with out saying that you should carefully pick a reputable kennel. It need not be fancy, but it must be clean and the dogs present when you inspect the facility prior to boarding your dog should appear well cared for and content in their environment.

You may be able to ward off separation anxiety when adopting an older dog. As outlined in the chapter on introducing a secondhand dog into your home, you should treat the new arrival as though it were a young puppy for a while to prevent behavior problems and damage to your home. If you crate your adoptee when you are leaving the dog home alone, he will be less likely to panic. Having room to race from window to window watching you depart increases the likelihood that a full-blown panic will erupt. As with a pup, give the older dog a special chew toy that will help occupy him while you are gone. It may take an older dog up to a year to fully adjust to a new home. Do not rush to wean your adoptee from the crate.

If you have a dog with severe separation anxiety, you may need to have your veterinarian prescribe a drug to help alleviate the distress until training and behavior modification can effect a more permanent cure. Keeping a dog permanently on drugs is not an acceptable solution. If your dog's separation anxiety is severe enough to require drugs, you will also need a qualified professional to help you with your dog's training and a behavior modification program to address the problem.

The first step is to stop the panic pattern of behavior and the destruction to your home. Crate your dog when ever he is to be left alone. Follow the same procedure outlined earlier for leaving a puppy home alone: quick potty walk, no big goodbye, toss bone and dog in crate, depart, no big hello, and a potty walk when you return. The next step, of course, is a solid foundation of basic obedience training. I have never seen separation anxiety in a well trained dog. This is because when training is done properly, it develops self control in the dog, the very thing a panicky dog lacks. Once the obedience training has progressed to the point your dog will hold a **thirty** minute down-stay without repeated commands or correction, in a very distracting environment such as your veterinarian's waiting room during busy office hours, start weaning your dog off medication if you are using it, but continue to crate the dog when left home alone. Once your dog is successfully weaned off the drug (he is not panicking when crated), you are ready to start weaning your dog from the crate if you so choose. Some owners with dogs that have suffered severe separation anxiety decide to stop at this point where a dog is comfortable being crated without medication because they do not wish to risk damage to their home by attempting to proceed farther. I prefer to try to wean dogs from their crates.

By the time you are ready to wean your dog from his crate, he should be in the habit of pacifying himself with the special chew toy you have been giving him when he has been left home alone in his crate. So when it is time for the big step of leaving your dog home alone uncrated, follow the same routine as before but do not lock him in his crate. Take your dog for a quick potty walk. No big goodbye. Just toss his bone in his crate but do not lock him in and walk out the door. **Leave your dog for one half hour only.** When you return, no big hello and immediately take him out for a potty walk. Yes, I know he just went a half hour ago but the excitement at your returning may cause him to need to go again.

If there is no evidence of panic while you were gone, in a day or so leave your dog home alone uncrated for one hour. Keep doubling the time you leave your dog home alone until you have achieved the necessary amount of time required by your schedule. During this gradual process of weaning your dog from his crate, if you must leave your dog for a longer period of time than he is prepared to handle, crate him! At any point there is the least evidence of separation anxiety, immediately go back to caging your dog **every** time you leave. Review the steps of the rehabilitation program and find out where **you** fell down in the process. Did you skimp on the quality of obedience training? Do not rush the program, done poorly, any attempt to alleviate a problem can make it worse! They are rare, but there are a few dogs that must always be crated when left home alone. Usually these are older dogs that have a long history of separation anxiety and failed attempts to resolve it.

If you must leave your dog home alone for extended periods, you need to provide for a midday potty walk or confine you dog outdoors in a secure outdoor kennel while you are at work or otherwise away from home. It would not be healthy for you to have to hold your water for eight to ten hours every day. Neither is it for your dog!

SHYNESS

Shyness is defined by Mr. Webster as easily frightened or startled, uncomfortable with and avoiding contact with others, distrustful, or wary. This fairly accurately describes the most common temperament flaw in dogs. Often a shy secondhand dog was brought to me for training and the owners just "know" that the dog was beaten in its former home because of its timid behavior. Maybe but probably not. Shyness is a genetic defect. This explains the other side of the coin, an owner that brings a dog for training because it is shy, and just cannot understand the dog's timid nature because he has had him since birth and have never struck or in any way abused the dog. All that said, there is an environmental component to the development of shyness as well as genetic. However, unless the environment of puppyhood was <u>extremely</u> neglectful and abusive, a dog is of sound genetic stock can be brought out of most, if not all, of its timidity.

I once had someone bring me a three-to-four-month old puppy she found abandoned on the trash heap at a dump. The puppy was so thin, it looked like a deflated football and so weak it could not move. She was just a sack of bones. I seriously doubted she would live. As I nursed her back to health, I came to call her "Lucky Puppy" because she was found just in the nick of time. Lucky Puppy was a manifestation of an incredible will to live. She was so incapacitated for the first month that I had to carry her outside and hold her up while she eliminated because so could not stand and she refused to soil her cage even with stomach distress causing vomiting and severe diarrhea! Lucky Puppy was so malnourished that all her hair fell out. After several months, Lucky Puppy grew a new coat and was up and around. She would never have surface beauty, but she shown from within. And here is the most amazing thing about Lucky Puppy, even though she was horribly neglected, probably abused, and left to die as garbage, she loved people! She did not have a shy bone in her body. I believe animals come into our lives to teach us lessons, among other purposes. Lucky Puppy demonstrated to me the undeniable role of genetics in temperament, and the power of the will to overcome apparently insurmountable odds.

Shyness is generally categorized as soft shy or sharp shy. Soft shy refers to a submissive individual that you could literally beat and she would not raise a hair to defend herself. While soft shy dogs are not a physical threat neither are they going to be the out going pet desired by most owners. Other dogs are what we call sharp shy, or fear biters meaning that when frightened they will lash out aggressively. Ninety-five percent of aggressive behaviors are rooted in shyness (please read the chapter on aggression for more insight).

No folks, it is not "all in how you raise 'em." However, a dog with a genetic predisposition for shyness can grow up into a normally sociable, loving pet in the proper environment. On the other hand, if shyness is predominant in a pup's hereditary make up, no amount of training and socialization may make it an acceptable pet. It is a matter of degree. So here my first word to the wise on shyness, DO NOT pick the retiring, little runt that hides in the back of the pen when you go to look at a litter of puppies because you feel sorry for it or because you have heard the fiction that they make the best pets! A knowledgeable breeder will have temperament tested the pups and be able to match the temperament of a pup with you, your family, and lifestyle. This, unfortunately, is a very rare breeder. Although a breeder may refuse to allow you to temperament test their pups, (and rightfully so because you could frighten a pup if you test incorrectly), educating yourself on the developmental stages of dogs and temperament testing will allow you to make a more knowledgeable choice. Read <u>The New Knowledge Of Dog Behavior</u> (see resource list) before you look at any pups. If after you get you new puppy home he exhibits shy behaviors such as startling and backing away, urinating, growling or snapping when someone approaches him, hiding, overly frightened of loud noises or sudden movements, **<u>RETURN</u>** the pup to the breeder. Do not use the upset of changing homes as an excuse for shy behavior. Yes, it is traumatic but most young pups adjust very quickly and even the slow ones within a few days. If a puppy is exhibiting shyness at a very young age it is genetic in origin, and will probably get worse as the pup grows, even with your best efforts. Keeping such a puppy is setting yourself and your family up for heartbreak.

If the pup you have selected is of normal genetic temperament, it is up to you to provide her with proper socialization to prevent environmentally induced shyness. Purina did a study in which one group of pups was raised with normal human contact and another group of genetically similar pups were raised without socialization with humans. All of the pups in the second group were shy. Furthermore, the critical stages for socialization were identified. These take place in the first sixteen weeks of life. Pups under-socialized during the first four months of life usually had some degree of temperament damage.

The eighth week of life is a critical fear imprint week. A pup traumatized during this week of development may suffer permanent temperament damage. In many states, well-meaning but uninformed lawmakers made it illegal to sell puppies less than eight weeks of age. And too many "breeders" (a true breeder is knowledgeable of developmental stages and operates accordingly) let pups go to their new homes during the eighth week—the worst time for the transfer! Ideally you pick up your new pup the day it turns seven weeks old. This is the optimal age for adjustment and bonding. Younger than seven weeks a pup will miss important lessons best learned from its dam and litter mates. The next best age to pick up your new pup is the day it turns nine weeks old. At nine weeks, the pup is past the fear imprint week but the clock is ticking for her adjustment and bonding in the new home, and all-important socialization.

So what does adequate socialization involve? Have your pup meet as many people of varying ages, sizes, colors, genders, and personalities as possible, both in your home and off your property! Take your pup to a new place to meet people and be desensitized to the sights and sounds of the world <u>at least</u> two to three times a week! You do not have to make a special trip each outing. Taking your pup on errands, to the grocery store, to the post office, to pick the kids up from school, is excellent socialization. Just take your pup out of the

car a couple minutes at each stop and allow him to greet some passerby. Take your pup to the school play ground or park to meet children.
Take advantage of stores that will allow dogs inside. If you have
friends that will allow you to visit with your pup, do so. Please be
courteous and do allow your pup to soil or damage a public place or
a friend's home. Clean up behind your pup outdoors. Thoroughly
potty walk your pup before visiting indoors and keep her on-leash
inside so she cannot get into trouble. Your pup also needs to be
socialized with other dogs and animals to prevent dog aggression and
predatory behaviors. Make sure the animals you allow your pup to
play with will not frighten or injure her and that they are current on
their vaccinations and healthy. Of course, your pup MUST be keep
up to date on its vaccinations as puppies are the most vulnerable. A
puppy training class taught by a qualified trainer is another excellent
way to socialize your pup, but a class alone is insufficient. You still
need to take your pup out to other public places regularly.

If your pup is not exposed to numerous environments, situational or "kennel" shyness may develop. A situationally shy pup
appears normal in temperament until she is removed from her habitual environment. Kennel shyness is a form of situational shyness that
manifests in dogs raised in kennels through the critical stages of
development that were not taken out of the kennel for proper socialization. In their kennel, these dogs appear to friendly and outgoing
but when you cart one of these unfortunate individuals home, they
are timid and cowardly, often extremely and irreversible so. Although
the first sixteen weeks of life are critical for socialization, it must
continue for a life time. If an older dog becomes isolated from people for an extended period of time, he too, may develop shyness. If
isolated from other dogs, a dog aggression problem may occur.

However it happens, if it comes to pass, if you find yourself the
owner of a shy dog and you are committed to doing the work to help
your dog improve to the best of his capacity, start with solid basic
obedience training. For shy dogs, it may mean life or death. If your
dog is extremely shy, find a qualified trainer to evaluate your dog and
to help you with his training. You may need to send your dog to
boarding school or private instruction before you can participate in a
group class. Proper training will build self-control and self confidence in your dog as well as giving you control over your dog. Estab-

lishing yourself as a strong and trustworthy pack leader through consistent training will give your dog a sense of security. Once you both have these tools in place, you will be able to begin socializing your dog.

If your dog is very shy, start the desensitization to people outdoors on your property. You may have to start by having a helper simply walk by. With a little experimentation you can determine your dog's present zone of comfort. Is he relaxed when a person is thirty feet away but begins to get nervous if they are at twenty-five feet? Start working stays at twenty-five feet or whatever distance your dog just begins to exhibit fear. When your dog is relaxed with a person walking by at twenty-five feet, than have your dog hold stays as a person walks by at twenty feet and so forth. Depending on the extent of your dog's shyness and the quality of your training, this process of desensitization may take weeks or just a few sessions. Do not rush and risk frightening your dog into regression. You are responsible to see to it that your dog has positive experiences with each little step of the way.

When your dog is ready for actual introductions, load a pocket with his favorite treat and head out into your yard. To introduce Chicken Little to a person (you will need a series of helpers who can follow instructions), put your dog in a sit-stay at your left side in the heel position. Instruct the person to approach the dog face-to-face. If the dog breaks the sit-stay, ask the approaching party to stop where he is or back up a step as you apply the sit correction. Once the person has been able to get within reach of your dog, have him offer the back of his hand, palm open, fingers pointing down to your dog to sniff. If this goes well have the person gently pet your dog and feed him a treat. If your dog has respect for your authority and sufficient self control built up through training, he can hold the stay and discover that being petted by a stranger is not life threatening and in fact, may be pleasurable! Be careful! DO NOT allow your helper to get his face near your dog's. Your dog may snap out of fear or an overly aggressive person may frighten your dog, undoing much of your hard work.

After Chicken Little easily accepts the approach and petting of a stranger in your yard, start working on introductions in your house. After introducing your dog to visitors, have him hold a down-stay near you where you can easily correct if necessary. Do not let your dog avoid further contact by hiding in a corner or another room.

The next step is to take you dog out into the world to meet people. In keeping with gradual steps you have taken so far, first go to a fairly quiet new area to practice introductions and slowly advance to taking your dog to more exciting spots. Again, you must guard your dog from too much too soon. Avoid practicing with people who cannot follow instructions.

With time, effort, and patience, most shy dogs can overcome their fear to a great extent and some completely. There are a few that even with extreme effort will never be acceptable pets. I believe that horribly shy dogs live a miserable existence in constant fear. In extreme cases where every possibility of reformation has been exhausted, these individuals may be better off recycled. The decision to end a life should never be made lightly. You may wish to consult with several professionals. The decision, of course, is yours and yours alone.

STEALING

Stealing food from table and counters can best be prevented by not feeding your dog from the table or while you are preparing food. Do not feed a puppy (under two years of age) or your adult dog any human food if you are having any behavior problems with your dog (see the chapter on Pack Psychology). Feed your dog from her bowl only. Do not allow your dog to lick the plates after dinner. In some dog minds, if it is OK to lick the plates on the floor, then it must be OK to lick them on the table too.

Often dogs that have not been fed from the table and counters are overwhelmed by the tempting smells of food. If your dog has not been inadvertently taught to steal (by hand feeding people food, etc.), it will be easier to correct the habit. In either case, correcting the food thief requires setting the dog up with Grannick's Bitter Apple. Leave the treated food on a plate near the edge of the table or counter. Now let Bandit discover that stolen food tastes terrible. Even though food stealing dogs don't sample, but wolf down their loot, eventually, either the aftertaste of the Bitter Apple, or the slight queasy feeling it produces in the stomach, will have the desired negative effect on your Bandit. As with any set up, the dog must not see you spray the food with the Bitter Apple. Wait a few minutes before letting your dog into the setup area so that the slight alcohol odor of Bitter Apple dissipates. We do not want Bandit to find out that stolen food only tastes bad when he sees you spray it or when it smells like alcohol. We want him to think that it tastes bad all the time so you effect a cure and can stop the set ups. You want the scene to smell and appear normal.

If you catch your dog in the act of stealing, scold her verbally while tracing a line from her eye to the loot. Do not make the scolding too frightening. If your dog is scared out of his wits, he will not make the connection between his crime and your upset. Then place Bandit on a down-stay for one to three minutes (one for pups, longer for older dogs) at the scene of the crime. It is embarrassing to be stuck at the scene of the crime. So the down-stay greatly adds to the effectiveness of the scolding. Do you remember getting caught with your "hand in the cookie jar" and wishing the floor would just swallow you up?

If you have one of those curious pups that jumps up on the edge of counters or tables to just check things out, place mouse traps along the edge. Set the traps when Bandit is not present and disguise the traps by covering them with a tissue. The tissue can be sprayed with Bitter Apple. If Bandit decides to swipe the tissue, it will taste bad. If you hear the trap go off, you can follow up with a verbal scolding and a down-stay as described above. This multi-layered approach is very effective.

No, the mouse trap will not injure any but the tiniest of toy breeds. Of course, use mouse traps, not rat traps, and even mouse traps should not be used in the home of toddlers or if you have cats that get on the tables and counters. The only dog I have ever known to get caught in a mouse trap was a friend's German Shepherd. The trap was not set for her but for a mouse. Lyka was attempting to steal the cheese with which the trap was baited. She quickly flicked the trap off her tongue, but she never ate cheese again for the rest of her life!

Other objects, such as stuffed toys, dish towels, pencils, remote controls (use a damaged one), eye glasses (use a cheap pair from the drug store) can also be treated with Bitter Apple. Remember not to let Bandit see you spray and wait a few minutes before allowing him into the setup area. Leave the treated target objects where your dog would normally find them. Doggie proof the setup area by putting untreated objects out of reach. Bitter Apple needs to be renewed two to three times a day. Set your dog up daily for at least two weeks running to effect a permanent cure. Two weeks is the length of a critical learning period for a dog.

SUBMISSIVE URINATION

Submissive urination is **involuntary** urination that occurs when a dog is excited or frightened. Commonly a problem in young puppies, they usually outgrow this stage. Most often this problem occurs in dogs of soft (submissive) temperament. The Cocker Spaniel is the champion of submissive urination.

If submissive urination is mismanaged, the problem may persist beyond young puppyhood becoming a life-long problem. There are two situations of mismatch of owner/family personality and temperament of a pup or dog that can result in submissive urination: 1) an overly domineering owner paired with a submissive dog (this owner will need to lighten up or find a gentler handler for Puddles); or 2) a boisterous household, paired with a soft temperament dog, (the household will have to lower its collective noise level or suffer a life time of wet shoes and socks or find Puddles a new, quieter home).

The key to successfully managing a piddler is to remember that submissive urination is **involuntary!** Your puppy is NOT in control of its bladder when very excited or frightened. Some pups just piddle for their family, some do it just for strangers, and some for everyone. We will look at all variations.

If submissive urination is not triggered, almost all pups will outgrow it. Submissive urination is usually triggered by owners in greeting their pup or during a punishment. If your pup wets when you arrive home, do not greet her. Immediately take your dog outside and give her a chance to eliminate voluntarily. Once she is empty, you may greet her casually, but avoid eye contact. After you have been home long enough for the novelty of your presence to have worn off, you may address your dog more directly.

If your pup or dog is wetting during a scolding, the punishment is too harsh. It may not seem so to you, but if a dog is frightened enough to involuntarily urinate, then it is also too frightened to be making the connection between your upset and its misbehavior. Of course, **you must never punish a dog for submissive urination because it is involuntary.** It is cruel and counterproductive to punish for something an animal has no control over.

As soon as your puppy is old enough (three to four months) begin basic obedience training to build self control and confidence in your dog. If taught to respond on one command every time in spite of distractions, training will help the submissive urinator enormously. I have often had a dog completely stop submissive urination by the time it finished its two weeks of boarding school.

If Puddles piddles when you have visitors, instruct company to ignore your dog when arriving, and to follow your instructions for a formal introduction. Take your dog outside to eliminate immediately before your company is due or immediately upon their arrival if they are unexpected guests. Then do a formal introduction by placing Puddles on a sit stay at your side and have your guests, one at a time, approach and casually greet your dog without a big fuss or making eye contact. You may wish to do the introductions outdoors in case there is an accident. Take Puddles inside on leash and place her on a down-stay near you. Once your dog has calmed down (after ten minutes or so), you may release her from the stay. If your dog becomes to rambunctious, put her on another stay. After the novelty of your guests presence has worn off, they may greet your dog a little more directly, but still should not make a hysterical fuss over the puppy.

Through the combination of confidence, self control building basic training and stopping the triggering of submissive urination, most dog will easily be reformed.

GETTING INTO THE TRASH

As with all problems, prevention is the best solution with trash raiding! The means of prevention may also be the best means of resolving an already established problem. Although it is not possible in all homes, putting the trash cans in a cabinet, under the sink or in a closet can prevent and cure the trash-raiding canine. Trash cans with lids are also a big help in preventing or ending this problem. Putting the trash up out of reach when it contains particularly tempting garbage is essential. Even with the best behaved dogs, trash containing meat bones should be put up or taken out to prevent that one-time raid that could prove fatal (bones can puncture intestines). You could also consider vegetarianism!

Once the trash raiding problem has developed, which sometimes happens in spite of one's best efforts, we have several corrections from which to choose. To correct the trash-raiding canine, spray the trash with Grannick's Bitter Apple when your dog is not present. Wait a couple of minutes. We do not want your Bandit to figure out that the trash tastes bad when she sees you spray it or when it smells like alcohol (the base of Bitter Apple—the odor of which will dissipate quickly). Bitter Apple must be applied every time you add a new piece of trash to the can or every few hours, and just before you depart home.

If the Bitter Apple alone does not effect a cure, you can try a little stronger correction. Mouse traps (the little ones folks, not rat traps) can be set in the trash and covered with a tissue spayed with Grannick's Bitter Apple. The tissue covering the mouse trap is necessary to disguise the booby trap. Otherwise, your canine genius will learn to avoid the trash when she spots the mouse trap, and will have a field day when the traps are not present. Of course, do not let Bandit see you booby trap the trash. And remember not to throw away the traps with the trash! When the intruding canine sets off the trap, the snap will startle her. Often the trash biting back is enough to discourage future raids. However, if you are within ear shot when the trap goes off, follow up with a brief nonviolent scolding. Tracing a line from your dog's eye to the trash will help her focus on her error. Then put Bandit on a one to three minute down-stay next to the trash can. The down-stay reenforces the effectiveness of the correction because it is embarrassing to be stuck at the scene of the crime. The down-stay next to the trash also forces your dog to think over what she has done wrong. Mouse traps must not be used for fragile toy breeds or in the homes of toddlers.

It takes a minimum of two weeks to break a minor canine habit. Therefore, you must set your dog up daily for at least two weeks running with either of these corrections.

For the bold and determined trash bandit there is a last resort correction. You can play the "This Can Is Not Your Can" overture in Bandit's ear. Catch your dog in the act and dump the trash on the floor. Put the can over Bandit's head and bang on it a few times and chew her out. Then leave the stunned criminal amongst the trash on a three-minute down stay. Of course, keep an eye on your dog and correct any attempts to break the stay. Do not let your dog see you clean up the mess afterwards ("maids" groveling on their knees do not look much like the pack leader). Do not use this correction on a shy, nervous, or an overly sensitive dog. If your dog is scared out of his wits, he will not make the association between the cause (trash raid) and the effect (ringing in the ears). This correction also should not be applied until all else has been faithfully attempted and failed. Unlike the set ups, this correction requires your presence. Therefore its usefulness is limited.

What is TTouch®?

The Tellington TTouch—is a method based on circular movements of the fingers and hands all over the body. The intent of the TTouch is to activate the function of the cells and awaken cellular intelligence—a little like "turning on the electric lights of the body." (Note! Click images to see larger view.)

The TTouch is done on the entire body, and each circular TTouch is complete within itself. Therefore it is not necessary to understand anatomy to be successful in speeding up the healing of injuries or ailments, or changing undesirable habits or behavior.

The Tellington TTouch is a specialized approach to the care and training of our animal companions. Developed by internationally recognized animal expert, Linda Tellington-Jones, this method based on cooperation and respect offers a positive approach to training, can improve performance and health and presents solutions to common behavioral and physical problems. It also helps establish a deeper rapport between humans and animals through increased understanding and more effective communication.

Using the star at a TTouch clinic for companion animalsUsing a combination of specific touches, lifts, and movement exercises, TTouch helps to release tension and increase body awareness. This allows the animal to be handled without provoking typical fear responses. The animal can then more easily learn new and more appropriate behaviors. By using the TTouch and a variety of other tools, like the Confidence Course, you can assist the animal in experiencing self-confidence in previously frightening situations. Even the most difficult problems are often eliminated. You can also learn how to apply the Tellington TTouch to assist with recovery from illness or injury, or just enhance the quality of your animal's life.

The Tellington TTouch can help in cases of:

- Excessive Barking & Chewing
- Leash Pulling
- Jumping Up
- Aggressive Behavior
- Extreme Fear & Shyness
- Resistance to Grooming
- Excitability & Nervousness
- Car Sickness
- Problems Associated With Aging

This gentle method is currently being used by animal owners, trainers, breeders, veterinarians, zoo personnel and shelter workers in several countries. There are many certified practitioners teaching TTouch around the world who can show you how to help you with your dog, cat or other pet. Please check the 'Practitioner Directory' to find your nearest TTouch Practitioner.

For more information contact:TTeam Training USA
P.O. Box 3793
Sante Fe, NM 87501–0793
800–854–8326 (M-F, 9–5 PM, Mtn. Std. Time)
http://tteam-ttouch.com

THE JOURNEY

When you bring a pet into your life, you begin a journey. A journey that will bring you more love and devotion than you have ever known, yet will also test your strength and courage. If you allow, the journey will teach you many things, about life, about yourself, and most of all, about love. You will come away changed forever, for one soul cannot touch another without leaving its mark.

Along the way, you will learn much about savoring life's simple pleasures—jumping in leaves, snoozing in the sun, the joys of puddles, and even the satisfaction of a good scratch behind the ears. If you spend much time outside, you will be taught how to truly experience every element, for no rock, leaf, or log will go unexamined, no rustling bush will be overlooked, and even the very air will be inhaled, pondered, and noted as being full of valuable information.

Your pace may be slower, except when heading home to the food dish, but you will become a better naturalist, having been taught by an expert in the field. Too many times we hike on automatic pilot, our goal being to complete the trail rather than enjoy the journey. We miss the details: the colorful mushrooms on the rotting log, the honeycomb in the old maple snag, the hawk feather caught on a twig.

Once we walk as a dog does, we discover a whole new world. We stop; we browse the landscape, we kick over leaves, peek in tree holes, look up, down, all around. And we learn what any dog knows that nature has created a marvelously complex world that is full of surprises, that each cycle of the seasons bring ever changing wonders, each day an essence all its own.

Even from indoors you will find yourself more attuned to the world around you. You will find yourself watching: summer insects collecting on a screen; how bizarre they are; how many kinds there are or noting the flick and flash of fireflies through the dark. You will stop to observe the swirling dance of windblown leaves, or sniff the air after a rain. It does not matter that there is no objective in this; the point is in the doing, in not letting life's most important details slip by.

You will find yourself doing silly things that your pet-less friends might not understand: spending thirty minutes in the grocery aisle looking for the cat food brand your feline must have, buying dog birthday treats, or driving around the block an extra time because your pet enjoys the ride. You will roll in the snow, wrestle with chewie toys, bounce little rubber balls till your eyes cross, and even run around the house trailing your bathrobe tie with a cat in hot pursuit, all in the name of love.

Your house will become muddier and hairier. You will wear less dark clothing and buy more lint rollers. You may find dog biscuits in your pocket or purse, and feel the need to explain that an old plastic shopping bag adorns your living room rug because your cat loves the crinkly sound. You will learn the true measure of love. The steadfast, undying kind that says, "It doesn't matter where we are or what we do, or how life treats us as long as we are together."

Respect this always. It is the most precious gift any living soul can give another. You will not find it often among the human race. And you will learn humility. The look in my dog's eyes often made me feel ashamed. Such joy and love at my presence. She saw not some flawed human who could be cross and stubborn, moody or rude, but only her wonderful companion. Or maybe she saw those things and dismissed them as mere human foibles, not worth considering, and so chose to love me anyway.

If you pay attention and learn well, when the journey is done, you will be not just a better person, but the person your pet always knew you to be. The one they were proud to call beloved friend.

I must caution you that this journey is not without pain. Like all paths of true love, the pain is part of loving. For as surely as the sun sets, one day your dear animal companion will follow a trail you cannot yet go down. And you will have to find the strength and love to let them go.

A pet's time on earth is far too short, especially for those that love them. We borrow them, really, just for a while, and during these brief years they are generous enough to give us all their love, every inch of their spirit and heart, until one day there is nothing left. The cat that only yesterday was a kitten is all too soon old and frail and sleeping in the sun. The young pup of boundless energy now wakes up stiff and lame, the muzzle gone to gray.

Deep down we somehow always knew that this journey would end. We knew that if we gave our hearts they would be broken. But give them we must for it is all they ask in return. When the time comes, and the road curves ahead to a place we cannot see, we give one final gift and let them run on ahead, young and whole once more. "God speed, good friend," we say, until our journey comes full circle and our paths cross again.

~unknown~

RESOURCE LIST

Getting In TTouch With Your Dog:
A Gentle Approach to Influencing Behavior, Health, and Performance
by Linda Tellington-Jones
ISBN 1570762006

How To Be Your Dog's Best Friend:
The Classic Training Manual for Dog Owners
by The Monks of New Skete
ISBN: 0316610003

The Evans Guide for Housetraining Your Dog
by Job Michael Evans
ISBN: 0876055420

The Koehler Method of Dog Training
by William R. Koehler
ISBN: 0876056575

The New Knowledge of Dog Behavior
by Clarence J. Pfaffenberger
ISBN: 1929242042

Printed in the United States
121245LV00003B/10/A